Amazon FBA

The Ultimate Step-By-Step Guide for Beginners to Make Money Online from Home with Your E-Commerce Business by Selling on Amazon and Make Passive Income in 2020

Ronald Anderson

© Copyright 2019 by Ronald Anderson- All rights reserved.

The content contained within this book may not be reproduced, duplicated or transmitted without direct written permission from the author or the publisher.

Under no circumstances will any blame or legal responsibility be held against the publisher, or author, for any damages, reparation, or monetary loss due to the information contained within this book. Either directly or indirectly.

Legal Notice:

This book is copyright protected. This book is only for personal use. You cannot amend, distribute, sell, use, quote or paraphrase any part, or the content within this book, without the consent of the author or publisher.

Disclaimer Notice:

Please note the information contained within this document is for educational and entertainment purposes only. All effort has been executed to present accurate, up to date, and reliable, complete information. No warranties of any kind are declared or implied. Readers acknowledge that the author is not engaging in the rendering of legal, financial, medical or professional advice. The content within this book has been derived from various sources. Please consult a licensed professional before attempting any techniques outlined in this book.

By reading this document, the reader agrees that under no circumstances is the author responsible for any losses, direct or indirect, which are incurred as a result of the information contained within this document, including, but not limited to, — errors, omissions, or inaccuracies.

Table of Contents

Introduction 1

Chapter 1: Get Started with Amazon FBA 9

    What Is Amazon FBA? 10

    Why Choose Amazon FBA? 12

        Most People Price Check with Amazon ... 13

        Amazon's 350 Million Products 14

        Amazon Prime Members Buy 15

        FBA Sellers See Up to Twice the Sales 17

        Amazon Merchants Are Common 18

    The Selling Truth 18

        eBay 20

        Amazon FBA 21

    Conclusion 22

Chapter 2: How to Have the Right Mindset 25

    Get Only the Best Information 27

        The Good 28

        The Bad 30

    Make Role Models of the Best Sellers 31

Create a Vision 33
Set Goals.. 36
Find Your Brand... 41
Consistency, Consistency, Consistency 44
Conclusion... 45

Chapter 3: How Amazon FBA Works   49

How It Works 49
   Send Your Products to Amazon 50
   Amazon Stores Your Product.................. 51
   Amazon Ships Your Product 54
   Amazon Handles Customer Service........ 55
   You Get Paid... 56
What You Do 59
   Choose Products...................................... 59
   Keep Inventory in Stock.......................... 60
   Market and Advertise.............................. 62
Conclusion... 62

Chapter 4: Advantages and Disadvantages to Amazon FBA...........65

Advantages 66
   Logistics and Shipping 67
   Discounted Shipping Rates 68

Management of Returns 69
Customer Service Management 71
Unlimited Storage Space........................ 72
Quick Delivery 74
Amazon's Multi-Channel Fulfillment (MCF) 75

Disadvantages 77
Fees and Costs.. 78
More Frequent Returns......................... 81
Difficult Product Prep 82
Trouble Tracking Inventory 82
Difficult Sales Taxes 84
Commingling... 85

Conclusion... 87

Chapter 5: Creating a Seller Account on Amazon 92

Getting Started 92
Individual and Professional Seller Accounts 93
Streamline Registration 98

Setting Up Your Profile 100
Account Info... 100

Notification Preferences........................ 102

Gift Options.. 104

Shipping Settings 104

Tax Settings... 105

User Permissions 107

Info and Policies.................................... 108

Feedback 109

Conclusion..110

Chapter 6: Product Research 114

Market Research 115

Define Your Audience 116

Survey Your Audience.......................... 118

Engage Your Audience 118

Prepare Research Questions 120

Identify Competitors.............................123

Profitable Products and Selling Mistakes 124

Common Errors 125

Product Parameters 128

Product Profitability............................. 130

Narrow Your Product Research Area.... 131

Select the Correct Online Tools.............132

Conclusion..133

Chapter 7: Niche 136

What Is a Niche? 136

Tips to Find a Niche 137

    Seasonality Slumps 138

    Profit Margins 140

    Competing Videos 141

    Product Dimensions..........................143

    Sponsored Products 144

    In Demand 146

    Niche Idea Search 147

Conclusion.. 151

Chapter 8: Suppliers 153

Wholesales 154

    The Four Benefits...............................155

    How to Make It 158

Overseas Private Label Suppliers............. 161

    Open an Alibaba Account..................... 162

    How to Negotiate with Alibaba 164

Product Launch 167

Conclusion..167

Chapter 9: How to Sell on Amazon ... 170

Create an Amazon Listing 170

Create an FBA Shipping Plan 174

Amazon Product Photography 178

Product Listing Optimization................... 180

    Product Title 182

    Product Features and Descriptions...... 183

    Product Results and Ratings................ 184

Create a Brand and Packaging 185

Automate Your Amazon FBA Business ... 186

Conclusion...187

Chapter 10: Amazon Ads 190

What Are Amazon Ads? 191

    Are Amazon Ads Worth It? 192

    Amazon Advert Costs........................... 193

    Self-Serve Ads vs. Premium Ads 194

Types of Amazon Ads 195

    Amazon Sponsored Product Ads...........195

    Headline Search Ads 197

    Amazon Product Display Ads............... 199

How to Optimize Amazon Ads 200

    Organize Campaigns 201

    Create Compelling and Urgent Ad Copy 203

    Create Specific Ads 204

    Bid on Popular Brands 205

    Experiment with Ad Formats 206

    Use Negative Keywords 207

  Conclusion 208

Chapter 11: Creating Your Brand 211

  Monitoring Your Amazon FBA Business.. 211

    Earnings 212

    Fees 212

    Seller Rank 213

    Order Defect Rate 214

    Perfect Order Percentage 214

    Customer Dissatisfaction Rate 215

    Pre-Fulfillment Cancellation Rate 216

    Conversion Rate 216

  Conclusion 216

Conclusion 219

Introduction

What was one of the first things you wanted to sell when you were a kid? Did you have a lemonade stand that went bust after two weeks, or did you sell baseball bats at little league games? Whatever kickstarted your selling career shows the true determination of a natural-born seller that was meant to take advantage of one of the world's greatest merchandise companies: Amazon.

Amazon has been around for over 25 years, and it only continues to build momentum. Once marketed as only an online bookstore, it was unclear if the company would survive the next few years against such large alternatives such as Barnes & Noble. The company was completely internet-based, which many thought would be the end of the website, but it only became more popular with the addition of new products such as music and clothes.

Some may not realize that the company that started off as an internet-based store for books was one of the first platforms to encourage outside sales. Originally called zShops, people could market original work or hard-to-find items. The idea exploded as more than half a million people purchased something on Amazon by 2000. Jeff Bezos was dubbed the king of e-commerce in 2001, just seven years after Amazon's launch.

From its birth until now, Amazon has acquired 40 companies, but its major commerce is now in its third-party marketers. Outside sellers make up more than 50% of Amazon commerce today, and that number is only growing over the years. Online shopping has become the norm, and Amazon is leading the way in sales, accumulating billions of dollars every year, and its third-party sellers are riding the train to financial freedom.

Amazon FBA was officially launched in 2006, so it is far from the newest selling platform, but it has shaped the path for other platforms of its kind, and it should be considered as the best service possible. Sellers can use accounts created with Amazon to sell their own merchandise with small fees collected by Amazon. With the internet growing in importance every year, selling online has never been easier.

But why would you want to get involved with Amazon FBA? Well, if you have a knack for selling products, feel as though you have always wanted an online store, or just want to try something new, Amazon FBA is one of the easiest ways to get started. From its promises of prime delivery to customers to its total management of your products as soon as they are delivered to the warehouse, Amazon has you covered. They provide a service unmatched by any outside company, and they make selling easier every year.

There are thousands, if not millions, of sellers working with Amazon to sell the very best products, but just as many fail as succeed. That is a harsh statistic. However, that does not mean that you have to be one of the many who have failed. This book is designed to give you the best possible advice for creating your own Amazon shop and to succeed brilliantly.

So what causes some to succeed where others fail? A large part of the problem lies with the lack of information that many have when they start selling with Amazon FBA. They are unprepared to calculate the fees associated with an account, and worse yet, they start to sell blindly, hoping that they will eventually find a product that is worth the money and time. This type of randomized selling is what gets most sellers into trouble. Instead of researching their products to find better alternatives and provide the best products possible, they assume their products will sell themselves.

If you found a little bit of yourself in the last paragraph, do not worry. It is not uncommon to feel this way. When starting with Amazon, many get so excited that they forget there is a lot of hard work involved in becoming a successful entrepreneur, but it is not impossible. In fact, it is so possible that many people have quit their day jobs to just work at their Amazon business, making much more than they had before.

This book contains information about all fees associated with Amazon FBA and step-by-step guides to get you through the most difficult parts of research and selling. With this book, you will be able to navigate your way through the internet and find the right tools to make thoughtful and informed decisions about which products to buy and when to sell.

If you have never researched before, never fear. There are thousands of others who have been in the same boat as you, and they all learned to succeed. Much of the information that you find on the internet is either incorrect or will prevent you from selling as quickly as possible. *Amazon FBA: The Ultimate Step-By-Step Guide for Beginners to Make Money Online from Home with Your E-Commerce Business by Selling on Amazon and Make Passive Income in 2020* holds the tools necessary for you to start your business and thrive. This book has taken steps to make sure that you are provided with the best information possible to succeed.

This book includes the basics of Amazon and all the information you will need to set up an account, which includes giving you the right frame of mind to make the most of your situation and business. Starting a company takes as much mental work as it does physical work, and this book offers a guide to get you started.

Just like all good books, we want you to decide which is the best option for you, so we have created a comprehensive list that shows all the advantages and disadvantages of taking the plunge into Amazon FBA. With the best information possible, we want you to make the best decision for your future.

This book also walks you through the basics of starting an account and basic marketing. Do not worry if you find yourself anxious about any of these subjects. This step-by-step guide is designed to make marketing and research manageable, if not outright fun. With the information you need to find the right product, this book then guides you through selling with Amazon and how to get your foot in the door to make connections with companies that may change your life forever.

There has never been a better time to start with Amazon FBA. People from all over the world buy from Amazon, making it one of the biggest selling platforms in the world. People are always looking for the best new product and the most exciting finds, which is what you can bring to their lives. Hold no reservations when it comes to your Amazon FBA experience, and let us start the journey of a lifetime!

Chapter 1: Get Started with Amazon FBA

A common view of salespeople these days includes used car salesmen and those disgruntled employees as the local supermarket that just want to leave and be done with their job...permanently. However, the sales' playing field is changing considerably, and much of it can be done right from your home. Whether this is your first time selling anything or you've been doing low-key sales for years, Amazon FBA is an excellent place to start your career.

Think of the last time you could make a full living working less than eight hours each day. Likely, if you have been struggling with finances, you have not had a day off in months, and the 40-hour week is more like an 80-hour week. It is not uncommon to have multiple jobs to finance a family, but it does not have to be the only option. Amazon FBA does most of the work and expects only products from you. They handle the rest. Both you and Amazon gain income from each transaction, and the flat rates associated with Amazon FBA mean that there are no surprises.

What Is Amazon FBA?

Amazon Fulfillment By Amazon (FBA) has recently hit the lists as one of the most exciting ways to create your own business today, but it may surprise you to know that it has been around for quite some time. Since its origin in 2006, Amazon FBA has grown to influence one of the most basic business models for fulfillment, decimating the previous variable-fee platforms to create a basis for clean transactions with little to no surprises.

Amazon FBA takes the hassle out of creating shipping costs and delivery fees by creating a flat-rate system that has been adopted by companies seeking a competing background. Amazon FBA, however, holds the standard for this successful business model, and it is becoming increasingly easier for third-party members to become successful through this amazing program.

Amazon ships products using its Prime platform. If you are unfamiliar with Amazon Prime, it is a paid service that provides discounted items and free two-day shipping for all products that qualify. This means that every product that is shipped from Amazon is already available in warehouses across the United States, Canada, and Great Britain, though it offers shipping of products across the world. So, a product distributed to your local Amazon warehouse may reach people from all over the world.

Why Choose Amazon FBA?

There are many platforms available to sell products, including starting your own website. Amazon may hold the golden business standard for third-party manufacturers, but why should you get involved? If you want to get a product out into the market and have never started a business before, Amazon provides a platform to launch products on a website that is used by millions.

While it is true that Amazon sells by the billions every year, it is also one of the most competitive arenas in the merchant arena. However, this should not discourage you from taking a stab at creating a successful business with Amazon FBA. Many have found their calling simply by marketing products on social media for their Amazon stores. Before becoming a seller with

Amazon FBA, consider the statistics below to inspire your journey to an Amazon FBA career.

Most People Price Check with Amazon

Nine out of ten people searching for products on the internet eventually steer toward Amazon. Price-comparison sites often use Amazon as a top competitor to monitor changes in price, and it is easy to see why. Amazon offers fast, reliable service that is delivered promptly for all Amazon Prime members.

Because Amazon has become so trusted, many people opt for choosing Amazon over other similar sites. Not only do the prices affect the way many purchase, but the excellent customer service drives people back again and again.

Amazon's 350 Million Products

Amazon's excellent service and easy third-party access have provided an amazing platform for third-party sellers. Amazon's goal is to provide products for every occasion. Its mission statement is to provide everyone with the perfect products with the best service: "Our vision is to be Earth's most customer-centric company; to build a place where people can come to find and discover anything they might want to buy online" (as quoted from Dayton, 2019). Everyday items, such as home supplies, and unique products are all displayed on Amazon's website, available to anyone.

This may seem daunting for new Amazon sellers, but it does not mean that it is impossible to sell on Amazon. Competition is at an all-time high, so it is especially important to do research into your chosen field.

Amazon Prime Members Buy

It is always good to know your market. When it comes to Amazon Prime, members are more likely to buy products than those who do not have an Amazon account. Why? The roughly $120 charged each year for the subscription comes with a number of perks including free two-day shipping on Prime products, access to entertainment such as movies and music, and early access to specific merchandise, just to name a few. Prime members are more aware of these products, as Amazon markets top items on its home page.

Members are also psychologically influenced by the great perks offered by Amazon Prime. Just as limited-time sales bring shoppers from all over to shop at a discounted price, Amazon Prime members also feel as though they need to take advantage of the perks that come with

Prime and spend more than those without memberships.

Since much of today's shopping is online, those who have access also like to take advantage of the free shipping. Items are more likely to sell online if customers can access the product with free shipping. Even if a product is listed as more on Amazon than another site that has paid shipping, shoppers will generally flock to Amazon, thinking they will receive a better deal.

With 95 million customers using Amazon Prime, the market for selling products has experienced exponential growth, and the new products added to inventory mean that the numbers will keep rising. Essentially, Amazon's large market has made it a hub for customer activity.

FBA Sellers See Up to Twice the Sales

Amazon Prime, the program responsible for the increase in sales in Amazon, is also the cause of the rise in revenue in FBA third-party sellers. Because people believe that they are receiving a deal by buying with Amazon Prime, average sales for third-party sellers increase dramatically. Coupled with two-day shipping, Amazon FBA merchants have the advantage of providing quality products that are more likely to sell.

Because the Amazon FBA draw is growing considerably, some products become overpopulated, and it is difficult to sell amidst the swarm of other deals. Creating a unique and useful product is the first step to creating a lasting career with Amazon FBA.

Amazon Merchants Are Common

Around 50% of selling agents from Amazon are Amazon manufacturers. That means that roughly half of the merchants on Amazon are third-party sellers. This should come as no surprise since Amazon's FBA business started in 2006. Though there is a lot of competition to sell items on Amazon, it is also the perfect network to discover unique statistics for your shop.

Becoming a merchant with Amazon FBA is easy, and there are many resources for people who wish to hear success stories. The all-inclusive site promotes small businesses and provides a platform for successful businessmen and women to succeed.

The Selling Truth

There are many places to shop and to sell products. Think about the last time you went online to find something of value that required research, like a laptop. Did you go straight to Amazon or did you look around at Facebook Marketplace, eBay, or a company site? If you are a smart shopper, you likely looked around at different sites to determine the best price available and then made a decision based on quality and ratings. With so many other online shops that sell much of the same things, it is often difficult to choose which option is best.

eBay and Amazon are two of the leading companies that supply merchandise to the customer, so why choose Amazon over eBay? There are advantages and disadvantages for both, but when choosing the perfect site for your company from which your business can prosper, consider the results for both you and the customer.

eBay

As a platform with a high percentage of third-party sellers, eBay is often the first thought when selecting the perfect company for an online store. eBay customizes the selling experience for both the buyer and seller by offering bids when specified and creating a customized store. It offers many ways to sell products, giving the seller complete control over the availability of products and specifying shipping conditions.

eBay is primarily dependent on the seller. This means that the merchant must create the store, ship products, and create conditions upon returns. The rating system within eBay can also be considerably harsh. If the product is not shipped promptly or the seller does not provide top-tier customer service, ratings may significantly decrease the profit margins within eBay.

The time spent on products to create a large following within eBay requires a large chunk of the seller's time devoted to customer service. As the business grows, so does the responsibility for customer satisfaction. For small businesses that do not expect much deviation in products, eBay may be an excellent solution to selling, but rapidly growing businesses should seriously consider Amazon FBA.

Amazon FBA

Like eBay, Amazon has provided a platform that supports customers and sellers, but its commitment to both the customer and seller is unmatched in any other online store. Think about eBay as a stand at a farmer's market. All the people who come to buy products are guaranteed with satisfaction or their money back. The merchant must both create the products and provide the customer service required to bring people back again and again. Think of Amazon, however, as a shelf at the local grocery market. Shoppers must go through the store to find the product. The seller's job is only to provide the product, and the rest is processed through the grocery store.

Amazon creates time for sellers by giving them a place to store products that are sent from various warehouses across the world. Once the product is sent to Amazon, the company handles the shipping, customer service, and return policies, all for a flat rate. Time is one of the most important commodities in the business world, and Amazon gives sellers the opportunity to grow businesses without the hassle of losing time, keeping people happy.

Conclusion

Amazon Fulfillment By Amazon (FBA) is one of the best ways to sell products, and its easy-to-use portal and service make it one of the easiest ways to sell merchandise. Third-party sellers make up most of the merchants on the site, proof that the popular platform is one of the biggest draws for outside sellers.

Creating a seller account with Amazon FBA gives merchants larger opportunities to grow businesses. The large market and the unique items in Amazon make it the perfect place to advertise, and those who put forth the effort are likely to see large gains in profits.

Though Amazon has promised a wide range of products and a means by which to sell them, is it worth it to consider selling with Amazon FBA? That depends on how much drive you have for your business. Just like any small or large corporation, items are not going to sell on Amazon or anywhere else if the seller does not put the time and energy into creating an avenue for moving merchandise.

Chapter 2: How to Have the Right Mindset

You've no doubt heard that a successful business depends entirely on the effort one puts into the business. This is true for any other type of achievement. People who set their minds on achieving a goal are more likely to succeed than those who do not have a set plan.

That is easier said than done, however. The way to develop the right mindset is through creating a pliable response, which is known as a growth mindset. Whatever obstacles arise, the mind is capable of either making the logical solution far better or far worse than the situation warrants. Those who believe that they either do not deserve or cannot move on from a situation often feel repressed and cannot succeed. On the other hand, a growth mindset allows adaptivity to situations.

Consider when you were a child. Were you told that you were smart or that you could gain intelligence through hard work and study? Children who are told that they are smart become easily discouraged when they do not understand complicated material, exhibiting a closed mind. Children who are told they can learn through hard work and persistence are more adaptable.

When creating a business with Amazon's FBA program, consider the adaptability of your mind. If you believe that you can compete with others in the highly competitive world of Amazon FBA, you can. If you believe you cannot, you are right. A growth mindset allows for change and does not remain focused on small inconveniences. Selling on Amazon FBA requires a constant effort to market and improve upon products already released. To make a living with Amazon FBA, the products sent to Amazon must be of high enough caliber to encourage people to buy from your business again and again.

There are challenges, however, to developing a mindset that encourages you to set a high bar for your business. Without a growth mindset, small setbacks can seem difficult to overcome. To prevent slumps that lead to a lack of interest and action with your Amazon FBA business, take the time to research and start your business off with a bang.

Get Only the Best Information

With all of the information on the internet, it is often difficult to discern which information is helpful and which is not. It may surprise you to know that most of the information you can get on the internet is either not accurate or points you in the wrong direction. There are only some sites and blogs that offer true information that will help to grow your business.

The Good

Keep in mind that the best information to grow a business with Amazon FBA comes from the source: Amazon. Amazon has set up various web pages to help you find the correct information about Amazon FBA, including shipping costs and fees, how to set up an account, and more.

Find information from reputable sources such as books and selected blog articles. Books about making money through Amazon FBA, such as this one, are often thoroughly researched to provide the best information possible. They contain information about getting started and how to improve business. Books that rely on market research and show the best ways to maintain an active commission are the best to acquire. Blogs such as Money Nomad, Full-Time FBA, and JungleScout Blog are some of the best resources to find specialized and general information.

Become more acquainted with the market by doing research in your chosen field. General knowledge of Amazon FBA is important, but knowing the market for the products you sell is essential. Every niche is different, so discover articles and books related to your product. The more you know about it, the easier it becomes to sell the product.

For example, marketing for a hula hoop is going to look different than marketing for an iPhone. Select the market that frequently searches for your product. Many markets may look for a hula hoop, but what makes yours different from the rest? Does it sparkle? Does it have lights? Information regarding what the market would want in a hula hoop is available online, and knowing what the customers want in a product will earn you a profit.

The Bad

As mentioned previously, most of the resources on the internet are not helpful in developing a business. A Google search may yield millions of results, but they are often unimpressive and incorrect. It takes time to sift through all of the less-helpful information, so as a general rule, avoid novelty blogs, promotions, and paid training. Though training may be beneficial to start with Amazon FBA, most are either scams or hold too much information that can only be accessed once.

Ads that are common on sites such as Facebook and Instagram are often wrong or lack key elements to starting a successful business unless you pay a large amount of money. Any subscriptions offered through social media or ineffectual media sites should be avoided. They often oversaturate emails with useless information, wasting time that should be spent on developing products and marketing.

Make Role Models of the Best Sellers

One of the best ways to create a successful business is to research the works of others. After all, the luxuries seen today are developed through research and improvement on the works of others. Follow instructions and generate ideas through careful study of best practices.

People who have grown successful businesses are great role models, and with the information on the internet, it is often possible to follow their steps to creating a lasting career with Amazon FBA. A great way to start is to research people who have used a style like your own to build businesses. People such as Steve Jobs and Bill Gates are common examples of people who have worked toward a goal and have achieved success. Books about successful people let you know how to find your place in the business world and are often the blueprints for success.

Becoming an Amazon FBA seller requires knowledge of the market, as mentioned previously. However, doing research on Amazon FBA sellers who have marketed and sold products similar to yours provides an in-depth analysis of what you need the most: a way to reach your audience. It is wise to avoid people who offer training at a price because free resources often hold the best information.

Create a Vision

Beliefs are the foundations for all actions in life. If you believe you can, you are right, and if you believe you cannot, you are right. Many believe that they cannot create a future while creating a web of excuse after excuse after excuse. The lies you tell yourself come true, and it is important to understand that beliefs are not reality.

Though beliefs change the reality around you, they do not define facts nor your future. For example, many believed that vaccines caused autism based on a fabricated study that has been disproven many times over. However, because people believed that vaccines were the cause of brain malfunctions, they passed on fabricated knowledge to people today. That belief has defined the reality of many, but it is not supported by facts.

Just as the belief that vaccines cause autism became a life-altering belief, so can destructive beliefs cause failure in your life. These limiting beliefs cause failure, not the statistics that guide the success of your business. Instead of submitting yourself to false beliefs, take a moment to criticize the beliefs that you hold. Examine your beliefs and discover what drives you and what hinders you.

Consider your beliefs. When it comes to selling on Amazon FBA, how do you view success? Are you only interested in a general scheme to sell merchandise, or are you considering the niche, market, cost, and reward? Creating a vision for your future business provides a pathway for future growth and development. Discover what you envision your business to be by laying down a plan to complete your goal.

Your greatest enemy when trying to complete your goals is you. Think about it. When was the last time that you accomplished a goal that you believed was impossible to reach? The only way to achieve a goal is by believing that you can succeed. This includes the necessity for frequent reality checks. How far have you come from the start of your business, and what mistakes have you made?

Though challenging, changing your belief system from one of success that is dependent on frequent success to one that accepts small mistakes is the first step to creating a successful business. Change the way you think about success by asking yourself the following questions:

- How can I view money in a way that will profit myself and those who work for me?
- What can I change to feel as though mistakes are simple consequences of hard work?

- How can I develop my skills to better serve myself and my customers?
- What can I do to experience the fruits of my labor?

Simple affirmations with a focus on how you can change your life to profit yourself and others help you stay on the right track and creates a goal that is easy to follow.

Set Goals

People who are successful take the time to set goals. Creating time frames for the completion of tasks that range from short-term to long-term keeps you focused on the importance of your future. But how do you set goals that will benefit both you and the company you are trying to create?

Successful goals are developed through the SMART goal system. Though it has now been around for many years, it is a good place to start when considering how to develop short- and long-term goals for the future. SMART stands for Specific, Measurable, Assignable, Realistic, and Time-Oriented.

Consider setting up your first sale through Amazon FBA. The sale must include a variety of extra tasks like finding your niche, paying for materials, retrieving materials, assembling materials, sending them to Amazon, marketing, and creating a system to automate your business. Any one of these is an example of a small goal that can fulfill the SMART goal system, but we will just focus on finding your niche in this example. The first step to completing the goal is to write it down by completing the SMART acronym.

S-Specific: Keep a goal specific by narrowing down your search with research. To sell on Amazon FBA, research the niche in which you want to sell and build on it. For example, the niche could be luxury towels, dog beds, or heaters. Within these groups, break down the information further by researching the best brands, quality reviews, and uses. You might even find that you will break down your search even more than you originally thought.

M-Measurable: Any goal must be measurable; success is measured. To create a goal that will stand the test of time, break it down into parts that will help you achieve your goal. For example, if you sell heaters, you will need to know the price of each unit, its shipping expectation, and its specifications, just to name a few. Research how much money it will take to get you started and set each goal accordingly.

A-Attainable: What is attainable for you may be unattainable for others. Likewise, while others might boast thousands of sales each month, you may only realistically be able to sell 25 units. The goal you set for yourself should push you toward a higher end goal, but it should not be out of reach. Creating an attainable goal means giving yourself the time and patience to achieve the goal. Without attainable goals, you will surely sink into a pit of frustration that is difficult to overcome.

R-Realistic: Though setting large goals is recommended, setting large, unrealistic goals prevents goal completion. Think about selling with Amazon FBA. If your goal is to sell one million products by the end of the first year, it is time to take a step back. Though it is certainly possible to do this, it is incredibly difficult, and setting such an unrealistic goal can cause frustration. Instead, break down goals into reasonable chunks. For example, if you are just starting with Amazon FBA, consider a realistic number of heaters you may sell. For the first month, set a goal to sell 25. At the end of the month, analyze your results and set a new goal for the future. Relying on statistics and past experience is essential to create a basis for new goals.

T-Time-Oriented: Consider a goal to sell one million products with Amazon FBA, but you do not include a time limit on this request. Frankly, it is unlikely to get done. Goals that have time limits not only help you envision your future, but they also inspire you to reach those goals by any means necessary. Selling one million products with Amazon FBA is a great end goal, but it is ultimately more helpful to divide the tasks into smaller goals. For example, give yourself time to sell your first few products. Find a groove that works for you and then base larger goals on data from the successes of smaller goals.

Find Your Brand

Developing your voice within the Amazon FBA community depends on how you wish to present yourself. For example, if you are looking to create a connection with single mothers, find the best products that will encourage them to buy. The voice you create within your business is the brand that will stick with you for years.

Your target audience is important to building your brand, and the way to stay motivated when selling to this market is to have a vested interest in its success. For example, if you are someone who sits in an office all day with little to no change in pace, you may consider selling exercise equipment that is useful when sitting all day. This market has a background that is similar to yours, and you will better understand the audience, bringing in more sales.

Create a mission statement that will determine how you intend to improve the lives of your customers. Mission statements keep you focused and drive you to improve. The more value you place upon your company, the more others will place, as well. They will expect service that is on par with the rest of your merchandise. Include in your mission statement the goals you wish to achieve and provide your own brand of motivation you can review whenever you need a boost.

Creating a list that discusses the benefits and key factors of your company is also a great way to build your brand. It is not easy to sell a product for which you have no love. Since this is your business and not one in which you are simply employed, take pride in your products. What makes your brand better than those around you? How does your service compare to competitors'? Though Amazon handles much of the customer service, keep in mind that it is up to you to market your products, so quick responses should be at the top of your priority list.

Find your voice with your company by exploring how you want to sell and to whom. For example, consider the voice of someone selling textbooks to a university. Likely, universities will be concerned with the material within and the ease of understanding. Now consider someone selling textbooks to a family. The family may also be looking for ease of understanding, but they may also be concerned with the applicability of the material, or they might wonder why they should buy textbooks in the first place. The way each is sold is completely unique, so discover what voice is unique to you and play upon your strengths.

Since you are unique, your company should be unique as well. Develop a brand with personality, and follow through on creative ideas. Customers who come back again and again often look at the creativity of marketing. Personalize each sale with subsequent thanks for the sales.

While finding a voice for your products and business, always be the first to advocate for your brand. Take pride in your business and promote your best work. Remember that you are the one responsible for bringing customers to your products, so do not be afraid of taking on the extra work to make your products shine. Constantly consider how to improve your business and remember to let others know how important your products really are.

Consistency, Consistency, Consistency

The only way to be successful in any industry is through consistency. If you are not seeing the sales you prefer, step up your game in marketing. If you are not receiving the products you sent out for, follow up and set up schedules to track your inventory. Consistency means finding ways to improve and following through on the menial tasks.

It is no secret that those who "keep at it" often develop their businesses quicker and see more success than those who do work irregularly. Using the motivational advice above, find a reason to want to sell, and building your business will become easier all the time. Develop a love for your products and provide a reason for your customers to love them as well.

Conclusion

Creating a growth mindset is important in building a business. When you allow yourself to see the mistakes made and prevent yourself from delving too deeply into frustration, you will see your perspective change rapidly. The only way to develop and change your mindset is through persistent devotion to yourself and your work.

The good information gleaned from the internet and books helps to create motivation when seeing the successes of others. A successful business through Amazon FBA is possible, and the best sources will let you know how to get there. Beware, however, of the bad information. Many blogs and forums on the internet are often steeped with bad advice that prevents success.

Find the best role models for your business by selecting those who have succeeded in a wide variety of subjects. They often pass along valuable information that is important to success. Develop a daily ritual to spend time in a book every day to gain more knowledge about their lives and build a strong background for yourself.

Beliefs that are destructive often make entrepreneurs feel as though they cannot achieve goals. Incorrect beliefs, such as those that cause frustration, are toxic, so develop a healthy relationship with your brain by giving yourself a pat on the back. The goals you achieve are necessary to keep consistent and realistic beliefs. Build practical goals that will encourage you to succeed.

Your brand is what people will remember when they buy your products. Often, when you give a valuable product, customers will look for your brand again to buy more. Never underestimate the importance of consistently keeping up with customers. People who respect your brand will expect consistent marketing and will build a solid relationship with your business.

Chapter 3: How Amazon FBA Works

Now that you have been properly motivated, how does Amazon FBA work? Amazon has been set up to create a business platform that is convenient for both the customer and the seller. Because of this, selling with Amazon FBA has never been easier, and when you have become used to the way the process works, you can set up an automated solution to basic selling.

How It Works

Many platforms today work with both the seller and customer to create the ultimate shopping experience. Luckily, Amazon's process for selling has been refined to provide easy access to third-party sellers. The majority of the work is done by Amazon, and you are responsible for getting products sent to its warehouses. All of the basics for Amazon FBA are broken down into easy-to-follow steps.

Send Your Products to Amazon

Though Amazon is known for its wide storage of items, it cannot sell your products if you do not send them to Amazon and set up the store with your Amazon FBA account. Amazon is in charge of holding your products, but you must act as any other online store and create a way for the products to sell.

Products sent to Amazon must be stored in one of the many warehouses in the United States, Canada, and Great Britain. Before you start listing and selling your products, you need to determine how much shipping will cost in the future. Changing the price of your products is discouraged, and fiddling around with prices due to the change of shipping information may hurt your online shop.

If you have a website already set up for your business (as many third-party sellers do), you will no doubt recognize the steps to creating a successful business. All information regarding your products should be listed with the product. Many people want to buy products that have a rich history or have significant information. Remember, if you do not have any reviews for your products, the best way to secure future buyers is to provide information they can use.

Amazon Stores Your Product

Inventory that Amazon receives from third-party sellers is categorized and placed in an organized fashion. They distribute packages according to size, packing labels, and weight. Some of Amazon FBA's fees are associated with the storage of your products in their warehouses. Think of it as renting a space in a large store. You will have the benefit of their client base, but you still need to give some reason for the merchandise to stay.

The fees for storing products depend largely on the weight, and each package is categorized in standard or oversized package sizes. The weights and prices are listed in Table 3.1 and Table 3.2 below.

Table 3.1: Fees for standard products with Amazon FBA.

	AMAZON FBA STANDARD FEES			
	Small Standard	Large Standard	Larger Standard	Largest Standard
Weight	< 12 oz.	12 oz. to 1 lb.	1 lb. to 2 lb.	2 lb. to 20 lb.
FBA Fee	$2.41	$3.19	$4.71	$4.71 + $0.38 per lb. over 2 lb.

Table 3.2: Fees for oversized products with Amazon

AMAZON FBA OVERSIZE FEES				
	Small Oversize	Medium Oversize	Large Oversize	Special Oversize
Weight	20 lb. to 70 lb.	70 lb. to 150 lb.	70 b. to 150 lb.	>150 lb.
Long Side + Girth	< 130 in.	< 130 in.	< 165 in.	>165 in.
FBA Fee	$8.13 + $0.38 per lb. over 2 lb.	$9.44 + $0.39 per lb. over 2 lb.	$75.78 + $0.79 per lb. over first 90 lbs.	$137.32 + $0.91 per lb. over first 90 lbs.

As expected, the larger the weight, the bigger the fee to store your products, so plan accordingly. You are in charge of keeping all products in stock. Amazon does not poke and prod you to keep your inventory active and available. You must keep track of all products sent to Amazon.

Along with initial storage fees, Amazon also requires a monthly payment for products stored. However, these are usually not unreasonable. They are subcategorized into the months required for holding the products. January through September, for example, are cheaper monthly than October through December. Table 3.3 displays these costs.

Table 3.3: Amazon FBA monthly storage fees.

MONTHLY AMAZON FBA FEES		
Month	Standard Products	Oversize Products
January – September	$0.69 per cubic ft.	$0.48 per cubic ft.
October – December	$2.40 per cubic ft.	$1.20 per cubic ft.

When a customer buys your product, Amazon works as the middleman and ships your product for you with no additional cost to you. Your inventory will likewise reflect the changes made with recent purchases.

Amazon Ships Your Product

Amazon's famous Prime shipping means that the customer will receive the product in one to two days. Since the product is out of your hands, you no longer need to worry about the shipping. All products shipped with Amazon are delivered through large shipping companies such as UPS. All you need to do now is wait for the money to come in.

Amazon Handles Customer Service

To those who are afraid to use phones, it should come as a huge relief that Amazon handles customer service...at least most of it. Amazon has developed long relationships with their customers. They follow up on products sold and make sure the product was received and is in good condition. They are also responsible for answering any questions related to the product, and they handle reviews.

That takes a lot of pressure off of you, but you are still responsible for some of the customer service work. Just as with any company, in order to grow your stock and retain customers, you need to seek ways to improve your work. The feedback you receive from customers is of the utmost importance to building an empire with Amazon FBA. It is your responsibility to keep customers satisfied with your products and offer new, innovative ways to improve.

You Get Paid

Some of the best words in the English language are the words "you get paid." As a reward for your hard work, you receive payments for the products sold. Everything in the transaction is handled by Amazon, and every two weeks, they deduct the fees associated with your account and hand you a large payout.

The fees associated with working with Amazon FBA are not often the first thought when receiving a payout, so it is important to understand that there are several fees associated.

Referral Fees: Amazon keeps some of the profit made from a sold product since they do most of the work. Referral fees differ for many products and are usually higher for items with the Amazon brand. For example, Kindles and Amazon Echoes are among the highest for referral fees. Amazon takes approximately 45% of the profit. However, for items not associated with Amazon, the percentages are much smaller. Items such as books and electronics usually do not exceed a 20% referral fee.

Variable Closing Fees: Though rarer than most fees, variable closing fees are flat fees that correspond to products such as books and DVDs. Be sure to research how much these fees will cost when deciding on a product to sell with Amazon FBA.

FBA Fees: Along with all the other fees, it should come as no surprise that Amazon charges an FBA fee that comes with selling products on their site. The fee goes toward selling and shipping your product, and in the long run, it is actually less expensive than packing and shipping the items yourself. In the end, the price for all the work that Amazon FBA does for you is just a few dollars. That is quite a deal.

Individual Seller Fees: There are two types of sales accounts of which we will discuss in greater detail in later chapters. Individual sellers do not have a subscription with Amazon FBA and pay $1.00 as a flat charge for any product sold.

Subscription Seller Fees: Subscription sellers are people who do a lot of selling on Amazon FBA. The fee to subscribe to Amazon FBA is $39.99 per month. That may seem like a lot, but if you are selling large quantities of products, this is the route to take. Instead of the flat individual seller fee, Amazon charges a monthly subscription that does not take out any additional fees for products sold. If you are selling more than 40 products each month, it is best to set up a subscription.

What You Do

So much of Amazon FBA is handled by Amazon professionals, so you do not have to worry about much of the heavy lifting. However, the work that you put into your business is the most important. It is up to you to supply products, keep the inventory in stock, and advertise for your company. Never think that simply sending in your products is the end of the road. There is a lot of work left to do to have a successful business.

Choose Products

Though the majority of strategies for choosing products is discussed in later chapters, it is important to briefly discuss it here. You are responsible for providing a product that others are likely to buy. Though it may seem like a successful venture to blow all your money on hippo decorations, you must realize that this market is very small. Hippo collectors may feel ecstatic to see your inventory, but it is unlikely they will see your product line if you do not know which markets to hit.

When choosing products, decide on a final product that makes you happy. That may seem corny, but it will actually help you market your products more effectively. Think about it. The love you have for a product will translate to your shoppers if you put in enough effort.

Keep Inventory in Stock

The inventory you put on Amazon needs to be continually stocked. If you plan on creating a product yourself, consider how many you will need to keep your business afloat. Customers that value your product also value its availability. Consider the last time you went shopping at your favorite store. Even if you went into the store with the expectation of buying only one thing, it is more than possible that you exited the store with more than you thought.

Impulse buying is one of the best ways to catch a customer's attention. When looking for a sweater for a niece or nephew, a customer might just come across your store of raven-themed miniatures. Often mistaking cuteness for class, the customer may think this is the perfect addition to the birthday box. However, if an item is frequently out of stock, customers lose interest and forget your product.

When selling items in many sizes and colors, always create a store that can supply at least twice what you think will sell. For example, if you create rings and sell them with Amazon FBA, do research about the most common ring size, the most popular colors for the season, and keep a supply handy. Sending just one of every style may create a "limited time only" sensation, but it will hardly encourage people to find your products in the future.

Market and Advertise

Like choosing products, this subject will be covered in more detail in chapters 9 and 10. However, before you even set up an account with Amazon FBA, consider the marketing that you can do for your product. Perform research about your chosen product, and develop a strategy that will bring in the right audiences.

Conclusion

The bulk of work to do with Amazon FBA comes from Amazon's end, which is highly beneficial to you. It allows you the time you need for creating and marketing for your products.

Once you have set up your store, send your products to Amazon through either Amazon's service or a common carrier like FedEx, UPS, or the USPS. Remember that the more reliable the shipping service you have, the more likely it is that your inventory will have a steady flow of products. Once Amazon receives your product, the product itself is out of your hands. Amazon handles the storage, shipping, and customer service that comes with the sold product. You get to reap the rewards of supplying products to Amazon without the hassle of dealing with customers.

When the inventory is out of your hands, your job is not done. Instead, you must still keep your business stocked with products. That includes regular shipping to Amazon and constant market research. To get the most out of your shop, you must know your audience and how they respond to different stimuli. Be involved with your customers. Be sure to answer any questions quickly and set up a rapport with faithful clients.

Chapter 4: Advantages and Disadvantages to Amazon FBA

Just as with any other company, Amazon FBA has many advantages and disadvantages. Be informed about your decision to set up a business with Amazon FBA by being aware of how each part of the company can affect your business.

Most businesses use Amazon FBA in conjunction with their own websites, and this is often because the business and exposure they get from Amazon FBA translates into their outside businesses. It is wise to have a stake in both a personal website and Amazon FBA account, though we will not go into further detail here. Suffice it to say that, before you fully commit yourself to selling on Amazon full-time, consider these advantages and disadvantages.

Advantages

One of the largest advantages of Amazon FBA is its accessibility. That means that anyone can access Amazon and select your products without fear of running into scams or internet viruses. Along with its highly marketable platform, Amazon also works with you as a seller to create products that are better for you and your customers. These, among many other reasons, are why many people opt for a business with Amazon FBA.

When considering the advantages of any venture, always consider how well you will profit from the collaboration. Below are more examples of Amazon's excellent service and the advantages that come with becoming an Amazon FBA seller.

Logistics and Shipping

Even if you have never owned a store before, you have likely experienced the grueling sluggishness and painstaking process that is mail delivery. Little inconveniences like the wrong stamps or the incorrect weight of a package can prevent you from making deliveries on time, and busy times, such as those around the holidays, can slow your business to a stop while you try to keep up with the demand.

When sending packages for your own business, you have to think about how quickly your shipping will reach the customer and what rating you will receive if a package is late. Often, when products get lost in the mail or delivery is delayed, you are the one that receives the brunt of a customer's wrath. The logistics with shipping packages can become exceptionally difficult to maintain, and if you are not experienced with shipping packages, some items may not be sent at all.

When you are part of the Amazon FBA family, you no longer have to worry about shipping or the logistics that come from untimely package delivery. Amazon has shipped billions of products, so they know the procedure. Also, if a product is lost in the mail, Amazon will take care of the customer for you, giving you an extra payment for the merchandise lost.

Discounted Shipping Rates

Not only does Amazon handle the shipping of new products, but it also provides both customer and seller with major discounts. The major mail delivery companies that work with Amazon offer major discounts because of the many packages they deliver. This means that both customers and sellers profit from the discounts.

Packages sent to Amazon in accord with Amazon FBA receive these discounts. Also, the two-day shipping that Amazon gives all Prime customers is a huge draw for customers. Those who come for the products may stay for the shipping. Its service is among the only of its kind. Shoppers with Amazon Prime subscriptions are more likely to shop, making your product line more accessible than ever.

Management of Returns

Returns are one of the most obnoxious parts of owning a business. Businessmen and women often have to shoulder the responsibility of paying for return shipping, refunds, and the cost it takes to send a new product, if you are lucky.

You may be surprised to know that returns are more common than you would expect. Clothing is often returned because online fitting is difficult. With Amazon's Prime Wardrobe, they handle returns often, as customers can send back clothing that does not fit or work for them. People also commonly return items that are broken or otherwise impaired. If a large chunk of your inventory has the same defect, the number of customers that return merchandise can explode.

Luckily, Amazon takes care of the dirty work for you when you sign up for Amazon FBA. The return shipping Amazon provides makes the task quick and easy, and you will see the changes to your store when the items are returned. Again, products are returned directly to Amazon, so you do not need to worry about additional shipping.

There is, however, a price to pay with return shipping. Amazon generally charges a fee every time a product is returned. The return fee is equal to the fulfillment fee, which you can calculate from Tables 3.1 and 3.2. Though that might seem like a pain, consider the advantages. Customer loyalty grows when they are offered free products or services, and free return shipping drives many shoppers to purchase merchandise on Amazon. When it comes down to the financials, letting Amazon take care of your returns really adds up in the bank. You will likely see a profit increase due to the number of products you are able to send in.

Customer Service Management

Dealing with customers is one of the leading causes of quitting jobs. Customers can be difficult to rein in when they have complaints, and it can become extremely discouraging to deal with people who do not like your product. Coupled with multiple returns, owning a business may not seem like the dream you believed it to be after all.

Amazon is one of the best customer service providers in the world. They have to be to get customers returning again and again. When you do not have to spend hours on the phone explaining why an order is not satisfactory, why not leave it to the professionals? With Amazon FBA, customers with complaints take their grievances directly to Amazon instead of bothering you.

Unlimited Storage Space

When developing an empire, storage space is one of the top necessities to keep your business running smoothly. Consider becoming a DVD or Blu-ray distributor, and your products are extremely popular due to the popularity of a recently released movie. To keep up with demand, you would need to either buy or rent a storage facility to take care of all your inventory. The costs for maintaining this storage facility may start to wipe you out, and understandably so. The more inventory you acquire, the greater the chance you have to make a profit, but it comes at a storage price.

Amazon has over 175 warehouses with over 150 million square feet to store your products (Amazon, n.d.). The only requirements to fulfill when storing products in the Amazon warehouses are listed in Table 3.3. Though there are fees associated with keeping products stored there, the price is far below what it would cost to rent a warehouse of your own.

Unlimited storage space is available for Amazon FBA sellers that are top in their class. Effectively, this means that if you are a high-profile seller with a high performance score, you can provide Amazon with as many products as you want. This cost-efficient approach makes it easier for top sellers to maintain high statuses.

Quick Delivery

As with all Prime-eligible products, shipping is free and sends within two days. The faster products make it to your customers, the more likely they are to buy from your store again. Customers come to expect fast shipping, so shipping with Amazon ensures that you will be on top of the game.

Quick delivery has advantages for sellers in other ways as well. For instance, since products sent to Amazon with the Amazon FBA program receive discounted shipping costs, sellers can quickly stock inventory if the supply is low. If you are new to the business and do not know how much inventory to send to Amazon, the quick delivery to Amazon can get you out of a pinch.

Amazon's Multi-Channel Fulfillment (MCF)

Though commonly confused with Amazon FBA, Amazon's Multi-Channel Fulfillment uses Amazon to store products but send via third-party sites. For example, many FBA sellers have a website outside of Amazon; in fact, 80% of sellers do. This means that they are getting business from another site. Using the same principles as Amazon FBA, sellers that utilize MCF send all their products to Amazon who stores and distributes products, but all is done through personal business channels.

MCF is entirely dependent on outside sources. MCF users often use other selling sites to promote and sell merchandise; eBay is a common platform for MCF use. Sellers build loyalty with customers by offering the same shipping and service requirements that Amazon has, but merchants are not responsible for what happens to the product after it arrives at the Amazon facility.

The fees for MCF are slightly different than for those expressly interested in Amazon FBA.

Standard-Size Products (Per Unit)					
Size	1 Unit Order	2 Unit Order	3 Unit Order	4 Unit Order	5 + Unit Order
Standard 3-5 Business Day Shipping					
Small: < 1 lb.	$5.85	$3.75	$3.35	$3.25	$2.20
Large: < 1 lb.	$5.90	$3.90	$3.40	$3.30	$2.80
Large: 1 – 2 lb.	$5.95	$3.95	$3.45	$3.35	$2.95
Large: > 2 lb.	$5.95 + $0.39/lb.	$3.95 + $0.39/lb.	$3.45 + $0.39/lb.	$3.35 + $0.39/lb.	$2.95 + $0.39/lb.
Expedited 2 Day Shipping					
Small: < 1 lb.	$7.90	$4.65	$3.55	$3.40	$2.41
Large: < 1 lb.	$8.30	$4.80	$3.80	$3.55	$2.99
Large: 1 – 2 lb.	$8.35	$5.35	$5.15	$4.95	$4.18
Large: > 2 lb.	$8.35 + $0.39/lb.	$5.35 + $0.39/lb.	$5.15 + $0.39/lb.	$4.95 + $0.39/lb.	$4.18 + $0.39/lb.
Priority Next Day Shipping					
Small: < 1 lb.	$12.80	$7.30	$6.30	$5.80	$4.30
Large: < 1 lb.	$13.80	$7.80	$6.80	$5.90	$4.80
Large: 1 – 2 lb.	$13.85	$7.85	$6.85	$5.95	$4.85
Large: > 2 lb.	$13.85 + $0.39/lb.	$7.85 + $0.39/lb.	$6.85 + $0.39/lb.	$5.95 + $0.39/lb.	$4.85 + $0.39/lb.

Table 4.1: Displays standard shipping prices for MCF users.

OVERSIZE PRODUCTS (PER UNIT)					
Size	1 Unit Order	2 Unit Order	3 Unit Order	4 Unit Order	5 + Unit Order
Standard 3 – 5 Business Day Shipping					
Small: > 2 lb.	$12.30 + $0.39/lb.	$6.80 + $0.39/lb.	$5.80 + $0.39/lb.	$4.80 + $0.39/lb.	$3.80 + $0.39/lb.
Medium: > 2 lb.	$15.30 + $0.39/lb.				
Large: > 90 lb.	$78.30 + $0.80/lb.				
Special: > 90 lb.	$143.30 + $0.92/lb.				
Expedited 2 Day Shipping					
Small: > 2 lb.	$13.30 + $0.39/lb.	$7.80 + $0.39/lb.	$7.30 + $0.39/lb.	$7.15 + $0.39/lb.	$6.85 + $0.39/lb.
Medium: > 2 lb.	$16.80 + $0.39/lb.				
Large: > 90 lb.	$78.30 + $0.80/lb.				
Special: > 90 lb.	$143.30 + $0.92/lb.				
Priority Next Day Shipping					
Small: < 1 lb.	$20.80 + $0.39/lb.	$11.30 + $0.39/lb.	$8.20 + $0.39/lb.	$7.70 + $0.39/lb.	$7.30 + $0.39/lb.
Large: < 1 lb.	$31.30 + $0.39/lb.				
Large: 1 – 2 lb.	$78.30 + $0.80/lb.				
Large: > 2 lb.	$143.30 + $0.92/lb.				

Disadvantages

Though Amazon FBA has multiple benefits and advantages, it would not be a true company if it did not have its own rules. The disadvantages associated with Amazon FBA are often included with the advantages. Though there are wonderful perks, many come at a price. The only way to determine if selling with Amazon FBA is the right fit for you is to weigh the advantages and disadvantages.

Fees and Costs

We have already discussed a majority of the fees associated with Amazon FBA, but there are others that affect overall profit within the platform. If products stay in Amazon warehouses instead of selling, they will ultimately cost you a bundle in sky-high costs.

Have you ever wondered how some people can afford the prices at which they sell their products? Some merchandise on Amazon sells for only $2.00, way below what most would believe is a success. In this case, most people would be right. People cannot earn a profit on Amazon by selling products at extraordinarily low prices. While it may seem as though selling thousands of T-shirts at $2.50 each will pay off in the long run, many fail to realize not only the basic fees but also those that are buried under a long page of script.

Amazon has provided businesspeople with a calculator that will determine all fees associated with their products. However, many of these fees are estimated, and you may not always receive a clear picture of the charges. When determining what products to sell and how many, always round up. Even if you will not have to pay the higher prices, this will give you the maximum rate at which to sell products.

Storage fees may also seem like a small price to pay for signing up with one of the greatest selling platforms in the world, but consider how these fees can build up over time. For instance, if you sell miniature lizards that weigh approximately 2 oz., you may believe that the deal you get from storing them on Amazon far outweighs the small costs of storage. However, if you believe that your porcelain lizards will be the hit of the decade and you send 1,000 figurines to Amazon, the price for storing your merchandise really starts to stack up. Even with the smallest weight class, it will cost you $690 each month to store your lizards, which only includes the months of January to September. As the holidays roll around, you will be paying $2,400 each month just for the storage.

Many people blindly start selling with Amazon FBA without doing research. Amazon FBA could seem like a rip-off if you are not careful about your products and market research. To prevent throwing away your money, take care of your inventory and keep an eye on marketing successes.

More Frequent Returns

Maintaining a strict policy on your website may prevent people from buying from your store, but offering fast and free returns increases the likelihood of more frequent returns. Since Amazon is known for its impeccable customer service, people are more likely to flock to the easy returns.

What does this mean for you? First, you will suffer the loss of a product that has not been sold, and you may have to continue to pay for its storage fees over time. Since you are charged for every return, the price for easier customer shipping also means that you are not seeing the same returns. If you are marketing a product that has size variations or inadequacies, you may see return fees build up quickly.

Difficult Product Prep

Though Amazon takes the guesswork out of handling products once they are received into warehouses, it does have rather strict guidelines for sending the merchandise. Any product that is not correctly labeled or sent to the right facility may be sent back at the seller's expense.

Trouble Tracking Inventory

When you run your own business, you can keep track of all inventory in and out of the shop. Receipts and order slips remind you who purchased what. Returns are handled by yourself or employees who know information about the customer, such as a phone number, email address, or the last four digits of a credit card. Shops that are run internally are designed to keep customer information for subsequent payments and to be a more personalized shop. It is not uncommon for a small business to know many of his or her customers by name.

Amazon FBA tracking, however, makes these connections much more difficult because, like most online stores, it does all of the above tracking for you. Much of your time as an Amazon FBA merchant is spent worrying about the products in terms of creating, shipping, packing, and making improvements. Though you may receive information from Amazon regarding product reviews, much of the personality of your business is exchanged for convenience.

It is not required to know the names of your customers, but when it comes to tracking packages, additional information is helpful for keeping track of orders. Amazon offers tools to make tracking easier, but it is still difficult to keep a handle on which orders went where and which customer left what review. If only one item was damaged, you may have to wade through multiple reviews to offer refunds or ask for product improvement, which takes a lot of precious time.

Difficult Sales Taxes

Keeping track of taxes can seem overwhelming for the smallest of businesses, but calculating tax with Amazon can become an absolute nightmare without help. Since Amazon is based in different states and countries, taxes vary. Even more frustrating, Amazon frequently moves products to different warehouses, changing the taxes on the products sold. Passing the road signs to even more complicated ground, you have to consider sales *and* shipping taxes. These also vary per state, and they might feel difficult to track with the range of different purchases.

Sales tax does not belong to the seller. Instead, the money collected from the tax goes directly to the states in which it is requested. But how do you keep track of which states need so much money? Amazon collects taxes for each state, but they do not give a clear pathway to set up payments to these states.

Various tools are set up to help you pay the right taxes for every state or country in which you do business. Amazon has its own section in sellers' FBA accounts that shows what the taxes are for the states in which you sold merchandise. Unfortunately, you will either have to be an accountant or have access to software that will help you sort out all tax information and lay it out in a readable form.

Commingling

Commingling with Amazon FBA allows you to bunch your products with other sellers'. When you see a product on Amazon, often there are buying options that allow you to select from which seller to buy. People from all over the globe can add to a single product, often providing a large selection of products. Commingling can offer you more contact with your product, but there are problems with this system that can lead to serious charges held against you and anyone else in the commingling product sphere.

Have you ever searched for a product on Amazon and received something that looked nothing like the photo and had none of the specifications that were advertised on its page? The product you receive is likely from another company trying to stiff you by riding the coattails of a more successful product.

Shoppers are taken in by the previous reviews of high-quality materials, and suddenly a flood of negative reviews may shut your shop down.

When participating in Amazon FBA commingling, you must be willing to take the risk that your high-quality products may not be the same as others. Even though the people reviewed your product and gave it a high rating, just as many, if not more, may try to make a quick buck. Always do your research when commingling, and provide an addendum to your product to ensure your customers receive the best quality and prices possible.

Conclusion

As with any company, there are pros and cons to setting up shop with Amazon FBA. Different products have different markets, which means that none of the same advantages and disadvantages apply to the same people. Always research your product and its sales on Amazon before deciding which product to supply.

Much of what Amazon FBA has to offer is automated, which means that you do not have to worry about the work done after the product is sent. Perhaps one of Amazon's greatest features is its customer service. Instead of spending time and money on shipping and customer satisfaction, you can focus on the most important part of your shop: the products.

Along with Amazon's Prime features that are included when you join Amazon FBA, you can also take advantage of its discounts on shipping. Not only do customers receive free shipping to their homes, but sellers can also take advantage of the lower costs.

Because of Amazon's quick delivery, it can handle a potentially unlimited stock to add to its collection. As products come and go into warehouses, you can stack more of your products into the shelves. Amazon's background of amazing service keeps people buying from its site, which creates a larger potential for your shop's growth.

Amazon's FBA program, however, also has several drawbacks that lead back to one thing: money. The fees and costs associated with Amazon FBA are, in our opinion, worth it, but it is wise to keep an eye on how much money you spend just keeping up your shop. Initial fees to send in products and monthly subscriptions to Amazon's great benefits may seem like the best deal you have ever received, but the charges add up, especially when sellers continuously add to their shops without receiving a correspondingly high number of sales.

Amazon's free return policy attracts many who want to try out a product with no fear of impending fees, but this often results in return fees that also build up regularly. Since it is more difficult to track inventory with Amazon, you may not be aware of which marketing strategy is failing and resulting in poor reviews. It becomes more difficult to keep everything in order when your business takes off, so constantly perform research.

The sales tax that differs with each state can be complicated and often requires a professional to sort out. The different warehouses that hold your products may change inventory at any time, also preventing easy tax information.

To make packaging easier, many choose to commingle their products with other sellers. However, if you are not careful, other sellers may create accounts that diminish the quality of your product, kicking the product out of

Amazon altogether. In the end, research into your chosen field and Amazon market can help prevent this.

Chapter 5: Creating a Seller Account on Amazon

Now that you have decided on a career with Amazon FBA, the next step is to get everything set up. Amazon's easy-to-use platform makes it easy to create accounts, and setting up the rest of the information is a breeze. This guide will help you to create the best account for you before selling your first product.

Getting Started

Amazon provides several ways to create a seller account that all lead to the same link: services.amazon.com. Follow one of these three ways to complete registration.

1. Navigate to services.amazon.com. Once there, select Start Selling and complete the signup process.
2. Navigate to sellercentral.amazon.com. Click on the blue Register Now button, which will take you to the services.amazon.com link. Select Start Selling to sign up.
3. Navigate to Amazon's homepage, amazon.com. Scroll down to the bottom of the page and find the section listed Make Money with Us. From there, select Sell on Amazon, which will send you to services.amazon.com. Select Start Selling to set up an account.

Individual and Professional Seller Accounts

The next step is to register as either an individual or a professional seller. Either way, you will receive payment from Amazon when selling goods, but the fees associated with subscriptions and listings are slightly different. So how do you decide which seller account is right for you?

A professional seller account is for business people who are in it for the long haul. If you plan to spend the majority of your time with Amazon and reap the benefits of a fully-functional business through one of the greatest online shops of all time, a professional account is right for you. A professional account only costs $39.99 for subscription fees each month, which means that if you are interested in selling many products through Amazon, the subscription is just a drop in the bucket compared to the money you can make selling products. Professional sellers are people who have experience selling and have sold more than a few products with shops of their own or have experience in the field. If you are not sure about whether you will need a professional seller account, hold off for a few months and give an individual account a try before fully committing.

An individual account with Amazon FBA will give you the freedom of selling with Amazon without the monthly subscription. With an individual account, you do not need to pay a monthly subscription. Instead, you are charged $1.00 for every product you sell. You receive all the same services that a professional would receive, but you are not locked into a monthly subscription. Most individual seller accounts are held by people who are only selling one product at a time or are just starting in the business realm. Selling smaller numbers of products eventually justifies the use of an individual seller account. However, if you start to sell more than you first thought, consider switching to a professional account. One dollar per sold product eventually adds up, and it is wiser to set up a professional account if you sell more than 40 products each month.

There are many other differences between individual and professional accounts, so how will you know which one is right for you? Consider the following differences to decide which account to start.

Shipping Rates: It only makes sense that those who have fully subscribed can access the best shipping rates from Amazon. Consider the last time you sold something on Amazon. If you were only interested in selling one thing, the item listed may have come with a standard shipping fee, which is usually $3.99 for standard shipping. Professional sellers with Amazon FBA are lumped into Prime's free two-day shipping, which gives them exclusive discounted shipping rates. If you send packages to Amazon frequently, you may consider moving to a professional account.

Listing New Products: Along the same lines as commingling, individual sellers only have the option of listing their own products with those that have been listed before. If you have recently set up a new shop with curly toe rings that have never been seen before, you must open a professional account. If you are new to the Amazon FBA selling game, you may find it beneficial to start with already-created products to jumpstart your career.

Gated Categories: The so-called gated categories available on Amazon are only available to professional sellers. These categories include "Automotive & Powersports, Collectible Books, Collectible Coins, Entertainment Collectibles, Fine Art, Gift Cards, Jewelry, Music & DVD, Major Appliances, Sports Collectibles, Streaming Media Players, Video, DVD, & Blu-ray, and Watches" (BuyBox, 2019). Though the list may seem small, it includes a vast majority of common items. To sell products in these categories, switch to a professional account.

Streamline Registration

Luckily, registration for a seller account with Amazon FBA is easy and can be completed quickly. However, there is some information necessary to complete the account, and it is best to have it on hand.

Personal Information: Just as with any registration these days, you are required to include personal information from which Amazon can recognize your account. This includes your name, phone number, mailing address, and email address. The information supplied helps Amazon determine which fees, costs, and payments are directed to your account.

Personal Bank Card: This could include a debit or credit card. Amazon's subscriptions and fees are processed as soon as the information is listed in your account and you have set up your first products. You must include a valid billing address and expiration date or Amazon will cancel the registration.

Tax Information: Amazon requires a tax identification number, which is usually associated with a social security number. Amazon must send a tax form to the United States IRS to provide evidence that you are selling products on their platform. Though they walk you through a 1099-K tax form, they are not responsible for withholding taxes for you. Once you start selling with Amazon FBA, it is your responsibility to send in tax information on the state and federal levels.

Setting Up Your Profile

Once completed, you can access your account at any time through the seller portal at sellercentral.amazon.com. You can change any information you would like, and you can adjust the settings to make your shop more accessible to you and your customers. Though it is not necessary to change any settings within the Amazon FBA portal, spend some time perusing its contents. There are likely some areas that require adjusting.

Account Info

All of your seller information is listed in the Account Info section of your seller account. If you need to change your name, mailing address, phone number, or email address at any time, do so here. The Edit button listed on the right side of your account information changes your information as requested.

One of the most important components of the Account Info settings is the Return Information subcategory. Do not become sucked into the fantasy that all customers will want to keep your products without exception. If Amazon is your chosen destination for returns, make sure it is specified in your account info. If you have not set up return shipping preferences, you may see a lot of products ending up on your door.

Make sure that your credit card information is correct on your seller account, or you may not sell on Amazon. Credit cards are set to expire, so inevitably, your credit card will change. If this does happen, change the information in your Account Info section. Keep in mind that Amazon may suspend your account for up to 24 hours if you do not notify them first. They will be able to anticipate the change in card number, and you may not experience the suspension.

Notification Preferences

It is a universal truth that once you sign up for anything, you are sure to be flooded with emails. Amazon is no exception. With constant changes in policy and updated terms of service, you may see an Amazon email more often than you would like. To change this, use the Notification Preferences button to change how many emails you receive from Amazon. You can specify what emails should be sent to you, and you may limit the number of emails to a manageable amount.

Remember that emails that come from Amazon are not frivolous. Those changes in policies or terms of service may negatively affect you, and you may see a deviation from normal practices. For instance, in March 2019, Amazon made an addendum to its previous storage policy. They offered a limited-time opportunity for sellers to test out new products and they would not be charged the additional storage fees. However, this limited-time offer was only available for select items and for only those who took notice. If you miss an opportunity such as this, you may find yourself paying far more than you realize.

Amazon also keeps a record of movement in your shop. This means if someone tries to contact you or there is an overwhelming issue with your products, you will be notified. However, if you do not have the proper notifications set up, you may never receive important emails. Though Amazon does keep track of everything that occurs within your store, you are responsible for keeping it up to date with improved products and better response times.

Gift Options

Amazon allows you to create gift options for your products. To sellers who provide products from their own homes, the option allows sellers to send personalized messages. However, you may need the assistance of a professional to help you set up this feature.

Shipping Settings

Amazon FBA sellers with professional accounts are free to set their own prices for shipping if they are not involved with Amazon Prime shipping. It is possible to make a tidy profit from charging high prices for shipping, and many use this approach. However, take heed of what customers will allow. For example, if you charge $60 for a product that commingled with other sellers, it is less likely that you will sell your product.

Customers are often convinced that free shipping will help their overall savings. While this is not the case, it does provide an opportunity to charge customers extra on the product with the illusion that they are paying less overall.

Tax Settings

To maintain a legal organization, remember correct tax settings are one of the fundamental pillars of a successful business. Why? If you take care of it right away, you will not suffer penalties or become confused with the changing laws. If you start with an alternative tax calculator at the start of your FBA experience, you will not need to worry about changing them later, potentially saving you days of work.

The state in which you need to apply tax information is up to your accountant to decide. At the very least, you need to pay state taxes for your residential state. Other states may claim the right to your taxes if you qualify under their sales tax nexus. A sales tax nexus is essentially a legal term for taxation of products or uses within a location. Think of it as the state charging you for using their roads and property. For example, if you live in New Mexico and use the storage facility in Arizona, Arizona may claim state tax nexus in association with your business.

Be aware that a sales tax nexus is connected to Amazon FBA because inventory storage and drop shipping apply to all Amazon warehouses. Since warehouses are located all over the United States, it is especially important to consider how much tax money has to be set aside in each state. Utilize the services of an accountant to set up the proper tax settings.

Tax information can become difficult to track, so an accountant is the safest bet when entering your tax preferences.

User Permissions

As an Amazon FBA professional, you may require employees to have access to some information regarding your account. As soon as you start hiring employees, you can add them as users to your account. Employees have their own login credentials and are only able to see exactly what you want them to see. This means that you decide how involved they are in your corporation.

Amazon has created a list of permissions that other employees are able to view, which range from unlimited to extremely limited. For example, if your partner wants access to your shared account, you can give him or her full access. An employee just responsible for sorting inventory may not have the same permissions but can still have access to the company site.

Be careful who you allow to access your account. If you decide to fire an employee, you must immediately discontinue their account on Amazon or they may gain access to your business.

Info and Policies

Once you start your online store, it is common to enter information about yourself. Though not altogether necessary, it does encourage customers to come back to you if they know a little more about your company. Use the About section to explain who you are, where your company started, and the qualities that set you apart from other sellers, which may include where your products are from and how you describe your style. Many customers like to know about the company from which they are buying, so take some time to hash out these details.

The policies listed on your webpage may include warranty or terms of use, though the area is wide open for any type of policy you wish to use. All Amazon products also contain an FAQ section, which provides an excellent opportunity for you to answer typical questions. Many sellers forgo writing policies because customers will typically ask those questions later, even if the policy is expressly given.

Feedback

Once you have reviewed all settings, you can begin to sell on Amazon. People from all over the world may order your products, and the reviews will start flooding in. Customers tend to base their purchases on the reviews from others, which means that one bad review—particularly in the early selling stages—could sour others to your products.

Amazon offers a way to calculate feedback, but it is far more useful to use a free outside source to find out what people think of your products. Sites such as SellerLabs, FeedbackFive, and FeedbackExpress are all excellent to start learning about your reviews. Be a step ahead of the game by having a marketing strategy based on feedback from your customers.

Conclusion

Getting started with Amazon FBA may seem like a lot to handle, but planning out which path you want to take before you even begin can prevent loss of time and energy. If you are just starting out and are unsure of what products you want to sell, begin with an individual account and base your decisions on the feedback you receive from Amazon and customers. If you already have an established business, consider choosing the professional account. Not only will it save you money on large orders, but you can all set preferences for shipping and new products. If you are serious about becoming a full-time Amazon FBA seller, consider the perks of establishing a professional account.

Though it is unnecessary to set up all the information in your account, your life will become significantly easier if you take the time to read through the options. Basic account changes and notification preferences may seem menial, but they could eventually save you a lot of time and money. Remember that, though you have the option to hide annoying notifications, most are necessary to becoming fully aware of changes and products.

Set your gift options and shipping and tax settings early to prevent future frustration. Much of Amazon is handled by the professionals, but correct tax and shipping settings may prevent inconveniences and lawful action. If you do not check for anything else, update your tax information and verify it with an accountant. You may be saving yourself from days or weeks of work by checking it before you start to sell.

As employees become more necessary with the growth of your shop, set up user information and grant them access to only necessary information. You can change the settings at any time, and disabling past employees' accounts is vitally important to keep a working account. While you are there, leave information about yourself and your policies so customers can learn to trust in the products you give them.

Always monitor the feedback you receive from customers. As we have mentioned before, marketing is one of the most important aspects of your selling account with Amazon FBA. If people do not know about your products, they will not purchase them. Keeping up with feedback can give you a leg up, allowing you to visualize what customers want to see.

Chapter 6: Product Research

The best way to get your business up and running is through finding and selling a profitable product. If you are working to do market research on your own, you will know that it is easier said than done. Finding the perfect product that will stun customers and provide the road to financial freedom is exceedingly difficult if you do not have the right tools, and most people do not.

So how do you find that magical product that will earn you that golden ticket? Market research is essential for distributing a product that people love. Think about an item you have been coveting or merchandise that you see others falling over. That is the beginning of product research: observation. Now, those keen powers of observation become wildly more valuable when you apply them to internet marketing.

Market Research

When it comes to finding the right product, there is only one rule: There is no right product. Many people spend far too much time trying to track down a product that is going to solve their financial burdens without realizing that there is no such product. It all depends on what is trending and how you market the product.

If you are new to market research, it may seem overwhelming to put in hours, if not days, of work to find out which products are trending. However, if you take your time to not only find products but also observe how others market products, you will be surprised about how much you learn.

Define Your Audience

You would not market a hunting knife to a vegan, and you certainly would not market giraffes to crocodile enthusiasts. To market efficiently, you need to understand your audience. Most people make the mistake of generalizing their products and simply marketing them to the community at large. However, if you want to see changes in your selling averages, narrow down your audience using the following audience types.

- Gender
- Age
- Location
- Pay Range
- Family Size
- Career Description
- Activity Levels

These are but a few of many descriptors that you can use to analyze the market you are trying to reach. Pick a group with which you relate. When customers see that you are willing to relate with them in the marketing scheme, they will be more likely to purchase your product.

If you are just starting out, use a spreadsheet to separate the characteristics of your audience, using at least 30 descriptors. Since there are many millions of people who shop at Amazon every year, you have to be specific about your marketing choice. Even if you narrow down the marketing funnel to people who have had smallpox and have ridden in an ambulance, you are sure to meet some expectations. Many marketers err on the side of caution and provide too general an approach to attract specific people.

Survey Your Audience

If you are just starting a business, use social media to interact with friends and acquaintances and use paid advertising to garner a following. Once you have a significant number of people to start a survey group, ask your audience what new or old devices they would like to see. Note the people who have volunteered to answer your survey. Do these people live in different locations, have different habits, or lie in different age groups? Take the information you learn from surveys to market a product that will guide you toward the people most interested in your merchandise.

Engage Your Audience

Once you have set up a following, promote your willingness to listen to their ideas. Most people are more likely to become loyal customers if you offer personal support. Provide avenues for easy access to your audience. If you are just starting, use your influence in your community to find out what people look for the most. Offer appreciative feedback when someone is willing to take the time to talk with you.

If you already have a solid backing in sales, you might already have a customer base from which to interview. In this case, offer incentives to encourage them to tell you how you can improve your products. Many advertisements on social media use this strategy to improve their results. Often, they present awards for people who give reviews of their products and thank those who participated.

When improving upon the performance of a single product, reach out to customers who bought it in the past and ask them for a review of your product. If they offer advice that could potentially help you increase sales or enhance the product itself, present them with newer versions of the product at a discounted price or free. Helpful advice, then, has an incentive for both you and the customers.

Prepare Research Questions

When participating in a study, when was the last time you had to answer a 45-question survey with questions such as "Why do you like me?" Chances are that you did not finish the study. There is a reason why surveys are short and sweet. People have always had limited attention spans, but with the constant distractions of today, it is even more difficult to convince someone to participate in a research project.

Prepare your research questions ahead of time and write out as many as you can. Do not worry, not all of them will make the final cut.

In fact, you should use this opportunity to combine like entries to create killer questions that answer more than one question at a time. Each question should be shaped to inspire the participant to think. Simple yes or no answers often tell you very little, and they often have the effect of leading a customer to think one way or another. Ask questions that will not only ask questions about the product but about the person as well. Use the following guidelines for the perfect survey.

Background Information: What can you learn about this person? You are better able to market to your audience when you know a little bit about them, such as the considerations listed above. Their age or location may not seem vastly helpful, but it can guide you to the right people when you market.

Awareness: What problems can you fix? When you are leading up to questions regarding your products, you need to understand the participant's point of view. What problems do they have that you can solve? If you are marketing for an in-home sleep apnea machine, ask about the person's problems with sleeping, their sleeping habits, other medical issues, etc. Each participant's response creates other possible avenues to people who would be interested in your product.

Consideration: What other alternatives and research has your audience explored? Understand your audience by looking into the same websites, books, and markets that participants have suggested. You can find new ways to improve your product and offer features that other products do not.

Decision: How did the customer make it to your market? Customers usually follow a winding line of research before settling on a decision. Whether they have made it to your store or you are simply looking for ways to market to an audience, ask the participants how they made a final decision on the product they purchased.

Identify Competitors

Whether this means stores in your local area or highly-respected internet brands, the only way to drive customers to your site over others is through identifying who is outpacing you in sales. Visit stores and online platforms to find out who these competitors are and how they market to their customers. Make the most of your experience by asking questions and exploring ways to improve upon their performance.

Many websites employ content marketers to help them boost sales. Why? Because their content usually answers questions and the articles contain search engine optimization keywords to drive competitors to their sites. Identify the top content competitors and make changes to your products that will satisfy most audiences. As a bonus, many people leave reviews for content writing at the bottom of the page that you can use to answer questions before they arise.

Profitable Products and Selling Mistakes

Once your market research is complete (or during your market research), it is time to pick a profitable product. Since there is no right answer when selecting a product, find something that you are passionate about and capitalize on the funds. The best way to sell a product is to find one you love and simply explain why you feel so strongly about it.

Common Errors

When selecting a product, most people get hung up on a lot of superfluous problems when finding a product, which makes selling impossible. Consider it this way: If you cannot find a product to sell, you will never be a great Amazon FBA seller. Avoid these common mistakes to get out of that slump.

<u>*Believing the Perfect Product Myth:*</u> If you are a perfectionist, you know what we are talking about. It can seem paralyzing to not settle for the best. However, if you only focus on what product will make the most profit, you will find yourself waiting for a long time. Your job is to find a product that will sell quickly, *any* product. After you have done your market research, you should feel at least somewhat comfortable with your options. Sell the product that hits you in the gut as the product you can market the best.

Information Overload: This book has already given you a lot of tips about what you should know and how to make the best choices with Amazon FBA. However, do not let this lead you into information overload. If you find yourself wondering how the rest of the world figured it out and you did not, it is time to take a break. Do not drown yourself in endless marketing techniques and possibilities. Take a chance with instinct after you have been given the best information possible.

Thinking Too Generally: Suffocating under the assumption that you must choose one category instead of one product often leads to frustration. If your question is whether you should focus on phone cases or fans, you are thinking too generally. Focus first on one product. Once you have found the product you wish to sell, focus on that product until you have mastered its marketing. From there you can start to build your empire.

Following the Herd: When one product explodes on the market, it is only natural to assume that you can make money from that product as well. However, consider the repercussions if everyone thought the same way: There would be an abundance of personalized kitchen washcloths with no homes. Pave your own way and make it unique to your circumstances.

Avoiding Future Forecasting: Future forecasting refers to a seller's ability to project his or her profits. This includes product purchases, fees, monthly costs, and projected products sold. Become aware of your financials before you sell even one product. Many believe that if they offer the lowest price possible, they will have the hottest-selling commodity. While that may be true, it does not mean that they will make a profit from selling the products.

Product Parameters

When selecting a product, be aware of the product's parameters. Remember, you want to find a product that will cost you as little as possible to store but as much as possible to sell. The criteria are ultimately up to you, but here are some suggestions to a more cost-effective product selection.

Start Small: When starting your journey as an Amazon FBA seller, remember that much of your money will go to fees if you do not sell your products quickly. For that reason, start with smaller products. Choose a product that is less than 15 oz to start. Shipping and handling fees will be much smaller for a standard-size package. Though standard shipment is for a package less than two pounds (or 32 oz), stay on the small side to avoid excessive fees.

Charge Reasonably: You might notice that many people who charge less than $10 seem to either sell quite a few products or hardly any, and the reason for that is two-fold: People either jump at the chance of a deal, or they think the product is cheap and therefore not worth their money. When charging customers for products, many people choose to sell products in the $15 - $100 range, which is highly reasonable. But, if you are looking to increase your profits and still provide an incentive for customers to buy your products, try selling products in the $20 - $75 range. The prices are still reasonable, and you make enough money to pay Amazon's fees while still making a profit.

Product Profitability

In order for a product to be profitable, you must sell it at a price higher than what you bought it. Of course, this is a no-brainer. But, when deciding at what price to sell it, consider the 3x rule. You want to sell your products at three times the amount for which you bought it. You want to cover the costs and fees Amazon charges and still come out on top.

Narrow Your Product Research Area

Now that you have mastered the basics of what you should look for, it is time to shop. With a wide realm of products to research and very little time to sell everything you wish, narrow down your product research area.

There are two potential ways to pick a product: finding a product within a niche and advertising through its market group or simply choosing a product and working from there. Both are highly profitable, but we will focus on the former of these two. Look for a product in a group that will allow you to both express your personality and relate to the people who share your interests.

If you are still unsure about what niche best suits you, take a look at Amazon's home page. The advertisements for products show that there is a good bet that those products are doing well enough to support the use of ads. Again, do not get sucked into the notion that everything that is profitable for someone else is going to be profitable for you, but they are a good guideline to show you which products are succeeding.

Avoid the restricted items in Amazon. In Chapter 5, we briefly mentioned the gated categories. Though it is possible to sell items on this list, spend the majority of your time focused on other products. These products often include extra permissions for shipping and selling that make it more difficult to sell in a timely manner.

Select the Correct Online Tools

When selling on Amazon, you will not only be using the internet for selling. In fact, use your resources to find the best material possible when selecting products. Plenty of Amazon FBA success stories start with finding a product that is worthy of their time and easy to market. To find more success, use the following tools.

StartupBros Workbook: StartupBros provides an excellent workbook to help you narrow down your search for products. It is completely free and offers advice about how to start up your own business. Their spreadsheet provides training to help you on your way to Amazon FBA success.

JungleScout Product Research Tool: JungleScout offers a paid training session with some of the best tools out there. They offer lessons, classes, and analytic tools, among others. They also offer an extension for your internet to help you find the best products. JungleScout is one of our top sites, so be sure to visit.

Unicorn Smasher Product Research Tool: This free service also helps to analyze sales with different products. One of its best features is its price. It is not as thorough as JungleScout, but it still offers a great extension for Chrome.

Conclusion

Before you even begin buying products, do some research into what the best products might be. Remember, there is no perfect product, so just choose one! To finally start your journey as an Amazon FBA seller, you need to have the products to sell, and you will never find one if you are too picky.

The market research you perform should make the most of the world around you. When you are looking for the perfect product, do not stop at browsing through Alibaba. You might find some products that you like, but many stop because they feel overwhelmed by the options. Ask your friends, neighbors, and social media following what they think about products today. Ask what they would like to see, how they would like their world to improve with a new product, or simply find something fun.

When conducting surveys, always pay attention to the questions you ask. Remember, you want to create a survey experience that is short but still gets you the answers you need. Find out each person's background to see how you should market your product, and use paid surveys for incentives if you are feeling ambitious.

When choosing a product, do not fall into common pitfalls such as wasting too much time narrowing down your search. Have some fun with the market research and find new online tools that will help you.

Make a profit on your products by following the 3x rule. Be sure, however, to keep the resulting price reasonable for your customers. They will not want to buy $300 products if they can find cheaper options with the same quality. Your customers depend on finding the best product for the best price, so be sure to beat the competition while still making a tidy profit.

Chapter 7: Niche

With all the products from which to choose, why would you want to sell within a niche? There are thousands of people spread across the globe who are looking for products that you are selling. Whether they are refined to canvas drawings of monkeys or are merely interested in finding a dog suit for the next furry event, everyone has a product that speaks to them.

What Is a Niche?

A niche is a subsection of a larger group. For example, if we were to use the same shirt example, you may choose to use a more descriptive term, such as a peasant blouse. This niche is a subcategory of the larger group, and breaking the term down into more descriptive terms makes it easier for customers to find your product.

There are millions of niches of which to take advantage, and now is the time to get started with your search. Take a concept for a product, such as the shirt, and narrow it down into specific subcategories. The more unique your subcategory is, the less likely that someone will have already developed a product for it.

Tips to Find a Niche

Since niches are so important to creating leads, it is important to spend as much time as you need to find the perfect one. Finding a niche is not an easy task, and more often than not, you will see the results for searched keywords are commonly used by other companies. However, this is the perfect opportunity to see what other competitors are saying and how you can become a cut above the rest.

Find your groove in a niche that is specific to your tastes by following products you are passionate about. You can become an advocate for your product while building your brand. Though finding a niche may be difficult, it is well worth the time. Below are tips to find your niche.

Seasonality Slumps

When searching for a niche, be aware that there are many seasonal products that will ultimately hurt your sales numbers. Consider, for example, selling a snowman decoration in the middle of July. The chances are that either you will sell none, or you will hit the jackpot with someone who is really excited about the Christmas season. On the other hand, if you sell a hot product such as exercise leggings, you will likely see much steadier results throughout the year.

When selecting a niche, select products that show the best results. You can easily find these results with a simple Google search if you know what to look for. Thousands, if not millions, of sites provide information on the best-selling products of the year, month, or week. However, remember not to pick only one website in which to do your research. The more information you glean from various websites, the more likely you are to find accurate projections.

Profit Margins

We all know that selling the most profitable item will bring in the big bucks. But how do you negotiate what your cost will be versus how much to sell? The 3x rule is an excellent start, but we will dive deeper.

Consider selling a pen on Amazon for $2.00 when it only cost you $0.05. Surely you are getting the best deal possible for the sale! However, consider the amount of money it takes to ship and keep the pens stored at Amazon. Though this might seem like a good deal, always remember to analyze how much profit you make after fees and costs. As a general rule, anything above a 15% profit margin is considered good.

Competing Videos

One of the best marketing tools is advertising videos on YouTube and social media. Why? People are more likely to watch a video than read a long post. Grabbing an audience with exciting videos makes potential customers more likely to buy.

However, there is a catch: Competing companies will be using the same strategy. To set yourself apart from the rest of the crowd, you must find a niche in which to sell your products. Large categories and general subjects deflect from your products and often create such a long list that potential customers have to wade through several hundred videos to find yours. This becomes exceptionally harder when they have the views that you do not.

Marketing a product in a niche is important to your overall sales because it narrows down your search parameters to bring customers to your product. Consider marketing for vanilla candles. When plugged into a Google search, the results yield nearly 500,000 results that range from making them yourself to advertisements for large companies. What does that mean for you? It means that you will have to create the largest ad campaign to beat out the already-established companies that thought of marketing for vanilla candles in the first place. Narrowing your search to vanilla cake candle cuts the number of Google video results by nearly half.

Be specific about the keywords that you use as well. Find words that most of your competitors are less likely to choose. For example, imagine you want to sell products related to your favorite monster (we are going to assume that is the manticore). When shoppers search for "monster products," they receive over 17 million results, but when they search for "manticore products," the video results reduce to around 13,000. Use your imagination when looking into your product niche.

Product Dimensions

As noted previously, the dimensions of your products are extremely important to consider. You must find a product that will be profitable but will also not weigh much. The niche you decide should properly reflect small dimensions.

If you are looking to enter the carpentry sales category, consider how much your product will set you back if you expect to sell only 3-meter bookshelves. First of all, you will have to pay for the oversized storage. Next, consider how likely it is that someone will buy your product. You may have spent over $500 bringing your bookshelf overseas, and it may take six months or more to sell the product. What is more, you will have to charge at least $1,500 to follow the 3x rule and pay for all storage and shipping fees.

Customers are no more likely to want to lug a large object around the house than you are to sell it. Most of the time, customers opt for smaller products on online sites. They are cheaper, and they are faster to ship. Also, smaller objects are less likely to be damaged (if they are naturally sturdy like our bookshelf example).

Sponsored Products

One of the most satisfying parts of research is finding a successful product that has an abundance of helpful keywords. Search engine optimization (SEO) is the leading cause of finding products. For example, if you are looking for a weighted blanket on a search engine like Google, you will find products that match your keyword on the first page. People all over the United States are hired to complete a simple task: Make a website more easily found in a search engine.

Because of SEO, creating a way to find your product is more difficult than ever. SEO provides a way for competitors to market their products, and if you are just starting out, you may find it difficult to market a product that uses many of the same keywords as others. For instance, defining your product by the keyword "shirt" may describe your product the best, but there are guaranteed to be millions of other entries for the same keyword. And that is where a niche comes in handy.

When marketing your product, use unique keywords to express your product effectively, and bring people to your product by giving them other options. Your niche becomes your corner of the market to which customers can come and make unique purchases.

In Demand

It should be a no-brainer that you want to find a product that is in demand, otherwise, no one will think to find it. For example, one of the biggest products of 2019 was leggings. If you look at Amazon's products, you'll notice that there are thousands of results for leggings, but only one stands out. Why? It is because the company listened to customers and offered them leggings that were reasonably priced and with the right material. Though leggings were a hot item, one company thrived more than the rest and created a demand for these leggings.

That brings us to another point: If there is no demand for a product, find a way to make it more desirable. Common household tools are often replaced because of breakage or cheapness. If you decide to make your living by selling spatulas, make them stand out among the others. Common examples may include turning everyday items into animals or creating indestructible products. What was the last time you ditched one of your tools for something cuter or of better quality?

Niche Idea Search

One of the most fun parts of creating or joining a niche is searching for products that fit within your scope. It is common to feel as though you have no idea what you want to choose, so do not become discouraged. Find that one product you have faith in and become its advocate. Follow these steps that will help you define your niche.

Identify Your Passions: We have rehashed this many times in this book because it is one of the most important ways that you can develop your store. Find at least ten products that you like and write them down in a list, writing down their pros and cons. Remember, you are trying to narrow down your search, so do not write down more than 30 ideas with the hopes that you will find one that suits your personality better.

Business is difficult, and starting from scratch can be extremely frustrating. Choosing a product for which you have no passion makes it that much harder to keep your head up. Think about what products you have seen in the media, on magazine covers, or down the street at your cousin Fred's house. Gain inspiration from people around you to narrow your search even more.

Identify Solvable Problems: Think like an inventor. Look at your everyday life and see what products you could create or distribute that would make someone else's life easier. What problems can you solve with the products you sell?

If you find yourself wondering if you can overcome some of the problems that arise from the malfunctioning product, it is a safe bet to pass on it. Problems arise in all merchandise, so selling a product you do not know how to use may result in more problems than it solves. For example, cheap technology does not often perform well after extensive use. You could sell the products just as they are, but you may see a lot of bad reviews and lower ratings. Stand firm behind a product to present the best quality you can.

Interview people around you and in online forums to see what problems the average person experiences in a day. Take note of the ages, locations, and statuses of all participants to get the most out of each survey. Note how you can make their lives better by providing them with a product that is affordable and worth the money.

Niche Profitability: After you have narrowed your search down to the final few results, look at the profitability of each niche. If you see pot holders selling for $5.00 each, it is a good bet that you will not make much money on the product, assuming you provide the same quality as everyone else. Become confident in your niche by seeing how profits rise and fall throughout the year. Use Google to analyze stocks for similar products to see if the companies are seeing increases or decreases for selling those items.

Test on Amazon: When you have finished your list, take some of them for a test drive. This means only sending some to Amazon. If you find that you gain profits from your chosen product, continue to send it in. Choosing the right niche may take several tries, but keep at it until you are successful.

Conclusion

When finding the right product for your Amazon FBA store, consider starting with a niche. You will find that you are better able to market to your selected audience when you know who your audience is. Market research becomes much easier when you narrow your results down to only a few options that fit your market.

When finding a niche that works for you, take your time to carefully study websites and Amazon itself to find products that are the most successful. Usually, the right product and atmosphere are right under your nose.

Consider what your niche can do for you. For example, if you want a big payout for a product that you adore, you need to keep in mind how marketable your passion product really is.

Understand that the products you choose are there to work for you, not the other way around. Do not get hung up on which niche is the most profitable if you do not recognize which product is the most profitable. Remember, you are selling products, not niches. Use your niche to market your products and use advertisements for the right people, but do not expand your operation before you know which product to sell.

Chapter 8: Suppliers

Suppliers will become some of your best friends as you continue within the realm of Amazon FBA. You cannot sell products that you do not have. So how close are you with your suppliers? With the tools you have learned in previous chapters, you are now ready to negotiate with potential suppliers.

Now that you have narrowed down which products you want to sell, the next step is to find the products you need. You can create your own or have them shipped to you, at which point you resell them. Since it is wise to look for inexpensive materials and products, many people order products from overseas. Wholesale sites are also common, but they often require buying in bulk to get a good price on products.

Wholesales

Creating a product base by wholesaling is highly effective, and it may promise some of the greatest rewards. If you are new to selling, however, it is probably best to wait until you have a decent following before you start selling wholesale products. That said, if you have a firm background in marketing and know how to sell yourself, this may be the best option for you.

Buying wholesale has four main benefits: Creating a connection with one wholesale company often opens the door for additional company connections, selling wholesale products often has a proven track record on which you can capitalize, you can often buy as many products as you want, and you can sell the same products over and over again.

The Four Benefits

<u>Sell the Same Products:</u> A successful business on Amazon involves finding a product that sells well and sticking to it. Essentially, if you find a wholesaler that is willing to work with you, you have the chance to sell the same products over and over again with similar results throughout the year. Others may consider this to be the holy grail of sales. If you can find a product that satisfies customers and the company with whom you work, you can maintain a fruitful business with Amazon FBA.

<u>The Great Track Record:</u> Unfortunately, many people sell inferior products on Amazon; just look on the internet for failed online shopping. This often results in negative reviews and an unsuccessful business on the Amazon platform. However, with wholesales, you already know the quality of the product from past reviews and sales information. With a

well-established brand, you are more likely to see sales. Shoppers like to stick with what they know, and if they have used that brand for years, they are likely to use it again and again.

For example, consider a trusted brand such as KitchenAid. They have had consistently high sales over the years, and their products have changed very little. They maintain a stellar track record and are among the top kitchen appliances throughout the world. Buying KitchenAid products wholesale and proving yourself an excellent marketer could mean that you would not have to sell any other brand.

Buy and Buy Again: It is often suggested that you have at least $500 in capital before starting a connection with wholesalers, though more is always better. Companies who wholesale products often require buyers to purchase a large stock. The good news is that once you have sold all of your products, you can always buy more.

Wholesalers keep their sellers interested through major discounts. Usually, you want to find a wholesale product that is 50% of the retail price, and there are companies out there that might beat those discounts. One of the hardest parts of wholesaling, though admittedly the most rewarding, is finding the companies that offer the best prices. Do your research to make the most of wholesale deals. Once you find your perfect company, stick with it.

Creating Connections: Often, companies that believe that you are a good selling partner will also refer you to a sister or like companies. This creates an avenue for you to expand your business over time. If you are successful at selling one product, your reputation will grow, and you will be more in demand from other companies. Companies look for people who have a proven track record, and selling for high-profile companies can land you those coveted roles as a wholesaler for notable brands.

How to Make It

With all of these benefits, it seems insane to try any other method of acquiring products to sell on Amazon, but searching the classifieds for wholesalers is more difficult than it might appear. Wholesalers are often looking for someone that can benefit their company. After all, they do not want to trust someone who will not get the job done, and understandably so. How, then, do you connect with wholesalers to convince them you are the right candidate for the job?

Step 1 - Choose the Company: If you are reselling merchandise, your product is the brainchild of a mother company. Though there may be many sources for the product you want to sell on Amazon, find its originating company. Often, the businesses you want to contact are struggling with one thing or another. There are several ways you can decipher what company you need to contact.

- Amazon ranking is higher than 100
- The product is not found on Amazon
- Products are sold by a third-party seller
- The company is struggling financially

Any of these options could mean that the merchandiser needs help selling their products, which is where you come in.

Step 2 - Communication: Companies that need help will likely welcome a call from a marketer. When selling yourself as a marketer for another company, always make a positive first impression, and that might mean that you need to get out of your comfort zone. The more contact you are willing to make with a company, the more impressed they will become.

If possible, schedule a visit to their company or find a time to talk with a representative. Face-to-face contact is highly desirable, and it is a nice break from the constant stream of emails most companies receive every day. The next best way to communicate is by phone call. Though not quite as personal as face-to-face contact, you are likely to be a step above the rest of the applicants due to that extra personal touch. Finally, if all else fails, send them an email. It is the least personal of the three types of communication, but it still shows some personal touch.

Step 3 - Prove It: You may have heard this many times on the childhood playground, but now is the time to take action. The first step to finding wholesalers to take you in as a seller for their company is to have the right background. Established sellers are more likely to get connections with wholesalers because they have experience growing companies, but that does not mean you cannot do it if you have no experience. Show the company what you can do by writing down marketing techniques and plans to increase their profit. Companies are always looking to improve their sales, so show them you can.

Overseas Private Label Suppliers

Another common way to get supplies is through overseas shipping. It is not surprising that Alibaba is one of the major contributors to these overseas products. Their supplies are cheap, and they ship at a remarkably reasonable rate.

Though Alibaba is one of the most popular overseas companies for retrieving supplies, they are also risky. The quality of the products ranges from well-made to complete disaster. Be careful about what you order through these sites as terrible reviews can prevent you from reaping the rewards of a cheap alternative. However, using materials from these sites to create better alternatives is an excellent way to capitalize on a good deal.

Open an Alibaba Account

As mentioned previously, Alibaba is a common site to purchase affordable materials and products. The first step to ordering from Alibaba is to set up an account. Follow these instructions to get started.

1. Navigate to Alibaba, select menu, and click Join Free.
2. Enter a valid email address and verify your account.
3. Fill out the basic information such as your name, address, phone number, and company name (the company name can be whatever you choose) and select Confirm.
4. Select a payment method from the choices of Trade Assurance, Gold Supplier, and Assessed Supplier (all are secure).

Make sure that you verify with your bank that all information is correct and that you have found the correct supplier for your chosen products.

How to Negotiate with Alibaba

Your suppliers are the bread and butter of your company, which means that you need to create a line of communication with them to get the best deals possible and to set up a trusted partnership. Though this might scare potential sellers off, communication with suppliers is absolutely essential to good business. When you communicate with suppliers, they are more likely to give you discounts and provide a good foundation from which you can build.

Send an email to your suppliers to get the ball rolling. If you are unsure about what your email should hold, use the following form letter as a basis for your communication.

SUBJECT: Supplier Business Prospect

Dear [NAME(S) HERE]

Though I cannot directly divulge company information such as monthly revenue and supply, my company would like to begin a supplier relationship with yours. From what I have seen of your company, I value the supply you give to other companies, and I would like to open communication with your company.

As a merchant, my company is looking to retrieve 100 - 500 units of [PRODUCT] on a trial basis. Should my company find the product acceptable and wish to continue our relationship, we will request 1000 - 5000 units of [PRODUCT].

We appreciate the time you took to respond to this email and ask that you let us know as soon as possible if this arrangement is reasonable to you. I look forward to continued communication between my company and yours.

Sincerely,

[YOUR NAME]

Remember that your suppliers are also business people, so they are looking for a professional relationship. Do not let this form letter scare you away. Adjust the wording as you see fit to work best with your business.

Set up the expectation that you are the negotiating manager first to set a precedent for future communication. Expressing this kind of authority makes sure that your message goes to the right person.

With your communication lines open, continue to negotiate with your supplier to find the best deals possible. Remember that you always want a sample of the products you are going to receive. These could be anywhere from 5 to 20 products at a time. Shipping for so few items will likely cost you, so expect to receive a shipping fee of $100 - $200. Of course, the higher priority the shipment is, the more money you will have to pay, so do not be surprised if you receive orders in the high hundreds.

Product Launch

When you receive products from both wholesalers and companies overseas, always remember to inspect your products. You do not want to send inferior products to Amazon as part of your first launch. There is a high possibility that at least some of the merchandise is damaged from shipping, so be prepared to either fix products or forsake them altogether.

Conclusion

If you want to become a successful Amazon FBA seller, you have to know where to get useful supplies at a good price. Using wholesale sites or overseas companies are both common ways to acquire supplies for your Amazon FBA business, but you must first know how to negotiate your way through good deals.

First, find a company that best suits your needs. This company must have both the supplies you need and discounts that make the purchases worth it. Companies are easily researched through Amazon and Alibaba, the two titans in the product supply arena. Make sure that you scout out more than one company to find the best deals.

Second, build a basis of communication with each company and establish yourself as a priority seller. Make yourself highly marketable by starting communication with high-ranking officials, and set yourself apart by knowing your product and business. After all the research you have done, you should know your way around your product, so use that knowledge.

Third, take care of your supplies. Though getting your supplies may seem like the hard part, remember that it is your responsibility to make sure that each product is Amazon ready. Alibaba may have some of the best deals on merchandise on the internet; however, the money you save with supplies is often outweighed by the time it takes to ship from China. Keep in mind that your customers come first, so always give them the best.

Chapter 9: How to Sell on Amazon

With all the information you received, you are no doubt ready to begin selling and taking that first step to your future business. Be prepared to shell out some more money when you are starting your business. There are certain package requirements required to sell products on Amazon.

Create an Amazon Listing

We walked through how to set up your Amazon account in Chapter 5, so you are well on your way to your first sale. The next step is to create a listing through Amazon. Work through the following steps to create the perfect listing for your brand.

Step 1 - Amazon's Seller Central: By the end of this book, you should be well acquainted with Amazon's seller central since it is the first place to start your listings. Navigate to sellercentral.amazon.com and select the inventory dropdown menu. The fourth item listed is Add a Product; select it.

Step 2 - Create the Product Listing: You have two options when entering a product: You can either choose a product from the search bar Amazon provides, or you can select to create a new product listing. When setting up your first product, select the create a new product listing option.

Step 3 - Choose a Category: Amazon provides a list of categories that describe products sold on Amazon. Take time to carefully go through this list to find the option that works best for your product. Though it is possible to list a gated item, it is far more tedious than simply choosing a product that will be uploaded immediately. Remember that gated items usually take up to 24 hours to approve.

<u>Step 4 - Fill Out the Required Information:</u> Generally, the required information for products includes the title, manufacturer, brand, and price. Do not feel as though you are required to have all the information right away. All information can be changed since you are not setting up a live account. You are just getting the information listed before sending products to Amazon.

Both the manufacturer and brand names listed can be the name of your company. If you are unsure about what that will be, just write something down. Again, you can change the information later. However, now may be the time to think about the name of your business.

The price listed is entirely up to you. However, make sure to look at the prices listed for similar items on Amazon. You want your price to be as close to the Amazon Prime price as possible, though producing a price that is lower is always the better option. Remember that you can change the price at any time as well.

Step 5 - Buy a UPC Code: A UPC code is the barcode you see on every product for sale in the United States. To become a businessman or woman, you must use UPC codes to mark the products you sell on Amazon. Unique 12-digit UPC codes are available on the internet, but be sure you are using the right website to get the best prices possible. BarcodesTalk and SnapUPC are two common sites that offer UPC codes at reasonable prices. Remember that when you buy in bulk, you receive a bigger discount. However, take your chances with a small amount before purchasing 15,000. Get your feet wet before diving in headfirst.

Step 6 - Product ID: With the newly-purchased UPC code, open the JPEG attached to the number and write the information down in the Product ID section. You can select what type of code the product ID uses, but the standard should be listed as UPC. Once done, select Save and Finish to complete your listing.

Create an FBA Shipping Plan

Once you have set up the majority of your product information with Amazon, you will notice the need to set up a shipping plan. Amazon FBA sellers get discounts with popular shipping companies when they sign up for a professional account, so now is the time to take advantage of those discounts. Use the following directions to set up your shipping plan.

Step 1 - Change to Fulfilled By Amazon: Within the Inventory dropdown menu, select the edit button and check the box listed Change to Fulfilled By Amazon.

Step 2 - Convert Only: A new page will appear after you have switched to Fulfilled By Amazon. In the top right corner, a button will appear that reads Convert Only. Select this button then refresh the page. Once the page finishes loading, check the Inventory dropdown menu again and select Print Item Labels.

Step 3 - Send and Replenish: The packages you send to Amazon may be individually packaged or sent in a large box; it is completely up to you. However, you will most likely save money on shipping if you ship all of your items together. To do this, in your Fulfilled By Amazon menu, select Send and Replenish. Then fill out the ship from supplier field. You can send all products directly to Amazon from your supplier, but it is often better to have the items sent from you. After all, you need to inspect your merchandise before you send it to Amazon.

Step 4 - Shipping Information: You may be required to fill out a Hazmat Review Form which determines what hazardous material is in your shipment. Unless you are dealing with highly toxic or otherwise dangerous material, you should not need to select anything other than NO in the fields requesting the type of hazardous materials sent. Though this form is not always necessary, it is wise to fill out the form just in case. Since it is likely your product is not hazardous, the form should not take long to fill out.

Find the dimensions of your shipping boxes. You are not required to know the specifications down to the millimeter, so give a rough estimate of each size. Do not, however, provide wild guesses. The space given for the dimensions of your products is measured in inches, so provide information that is somewhat accurate down to the inch. Also include the number of items in your box.

Next, Amazon will request information regarding prep. They essentially want to know if Amazon will need to do any of the prep work. Since you should be inspecting all of your products, the answer should be NO. Do not rack up extra fees by making Amazon do your prep for you. All the labels should be completed by the manufacturer, which is you. When filling out this section, make sure to mention that you will be doing all of the work.

Step 5 - Shipment Options: When asked how you will ship the items, fill out the company you will use to ship your products. The most common choice is UPS for its speed and reliability, but USPS often offers cheaper options, so choose wisely.

Amazon Product Photography

Photographs are required when listing a product, so be sure to have all the photographs you need before you start the listing. Create the best product by giving customers the best information about your product through images. One of the most important parts of a product is its photography. Think about the last product you bought online. Would you have bought it if there had not been a photograph attached to it? Customers often believe photos are the make-or-break factors of a product. For example, many search for vehicles online, but few even click on ads for vehicles with less than five photos.

Shoppers want to see what they are buying, and that goes for any product online. The best bet you have for selling a product is to provide the customer with as much detail as you can. If you have a limited budget for photos, consider reducing the amount, but try to stay above three total photos for each product.

Many companies offer professional photography for all products you wish to sell, and many of them have decent prices for the work. For instance, Product Photography offers services that are as low as $24 per image. Additional product photography sites often offer these kinds of deals, but you will have to shop around to find the prices that are right for you.

Amazon also provides professional product photography for any and all of your merchandise, but it does come at a cost. Five photos are priced at $250, so it does require some financial backing to get the best bang for your buck. However, if you can afford it, professional photography by Amazon may be worth it.

If you feel a tug at your purse strings, you can always take the photos yourself. There are thousands of online videos to help you create your own professional photos. Try to provide photos that show as much detail as possible for the best results. Also, local photographers are likely to give excellent prices for taking photos. Consider giving local businesses a chance with the same excellent results.

Product Listing Optimization

Though you may have the best product on the market and offer the best prices, without product listing optimization, it is unlikely that you will receive as many views as you hope. Fortunately, there are several ways to improve your product listing so you can achieve the best possible results.

Product listing optimization is the process of making your product the highest rated of its kind. Once you have created the listing, just how important is it to create a product that is optimized? The three main reasons to optimize a product are to increase your overall rankings, to bring people to your product, and to ultimately grow sales. So, you could say that product listing optimization is one of the most important parts of listing a product on Amazon. Optimization is a worthy way to spend your time, but we want to create the experience easier for you. Here are some of the key ways to optimize your product listing.

Product Title

When was the last time you purchased a product that had a title like "Goo For Sale"? Though slime has become increasingly popular over the years, that does not mean that you should advertise it as "goo." Think about a name for the title that will inspire people to find what they are looking for.

Chapter 7's discussion of SEO is the perfect introduction to creating a product title that will grab attention. Remember, you want to create a title that is descriptive of your product while maintaining a specific nature. For example, your product title for packaged slime should contain the word "slime" to better direct people to your product, but you can provide greater optimization by adding a descriptor. If your slime has blues and purples with glitter, you may market it as "Galaxy Slime." This will narrow down potential searches and create an attention-grabbing name for potential buyers.

Product Features and Descriptions

As has been discussed multiple times in this book, it is essential to create a listing with a product that has a lot of descriptors. In your description settings, add product dimensions, type of material, styles, and any other descriptors you find necessary. Arrange these into bullet points for easier reading.

Put yourself in the customer's shoes. How will they know that they are buying the right product? If you are unsure of how much information you should add about your product, put your shoes on the customer. What does this mean? Create descriptions with enough detail that your customer can visualize what the product actually feels like. Show customers how much they will love your product by virtually placing them in the same room as your product. Many believe that online shopping will never overtake the experience of physically shopping, so create the moment for them by bringing buyers an unforgettable experience.

Product Results and Ratings

What about your product makes it stand apart from the rest? Many shoppers buy products looking to improve some aspect of their lives. Your product should describe the results that it achieves. Many people are willing to spend a large sum of money for a product that actually works. Encourage reviews to bring people back again and again.

Consider the Indian Healing Clay product on Amazon that has received almost 25,000 ratings with an average star rating of 4.4 out of 5. This simple clay, once mixed with water or apple cider vinegar, is an effective acne reducer. Chances are that you have never seen an ad for this product, but it is still one of the most popular products on the Amazon market. The product has the right balance of cost-effectiveness and positive product reviews that have caused it to make the lists of some of the most popular blogs. They use many descriptors but mostly use the strength of the product to speak for itself.

Create a Brand and Packaging

One of the best ways to sell products is to provide excellent graphics. This applies to both your logo and product designs. Sites like Freeeup and Fiverr are often the best to find talented graphic designers to help you build your brand. Make use of their expertise within a healthy budget for anything you need.

Another way to ensure you make the most out of your product is by creating a packaging design that is unique to you. Many people are impressed by the effort sellers put into small additions. Consider including a thank you note or any other letter within your product to encourage customers to think of you again. In your letter, use your logo or other packaging design to add personality.

Automate Your Amazon FBA Business

Many third-party companies do much of the work for you so you can focus on keeping up your branding through marketing and optimization. This is your business, so automating everything is up to you. You will likely have to shell out money that would otherwise go to your own funds, but other companies save you the trouble of inspecting and shipping products that come in from China and wholesalers.

Third-party companies such as [FBA Inspection](#) are commonly used to make your life easier. They offer low prices for each product you would like inspected. Amazon FBA does not allow suppliers to do the inspection for you, so you need to rely on either yourself or a middleman to complete the work. Note that you should only consider this option after you have everything set up in Amazon. You might find yourself paying too much out of pocket to make any profit if you are not comfortably set with your sales.

Conclusion

Before you even sell your products, set up a listing on Amazon. Make sure that the listing is not live before it is published. While setting general information, consider the best way to ship your products to Amazon. Utilize common shipping companies associated with Amazon to get the best discounts and make shipping faster.

When creating listings for Amazon, always remember to use the tools around you to get the most out of your listings. Optimized simple features that Amazon requires on each of its listings could springboard you into a more comfortable market. Taking the time to optimize your listings through selecting unique product titles, relating product features and descriptions effectively, and utilizing Amazon results and ratings will provide a basis for a highly-visited store.

Consider the costs of an effective Amazon shop. If you want to make the most out of every listing, hire the best graphic designers and photographers to make your products pop. Remember, your aim is to create a listing that is pleasing to the eye. High ratings and many reviews are common reasons for page visits, so encourage customers to leave reviews of your products.

Once you have finished setting up your products and have some selling experience under your belt, consider automating your business. You can pay others to inspect your products for you so you can focus on producing the best marketing information possible. Since this is your company, use your best judgment concerning costs to optimize your income while making your life easier.

Chapter 10: Amazon Ads

Whether you work as a marketer or you have been living under a rock, it is almost impossible to miss the ads that pop up on the computer, on billboards, or in any written material. Applications have been made to block ads on your phone or computer because they have become so prevalent in today's society. Why? Because they work.

Customers not only expect to see ads on online shopping sites, but they often respond well to the stimulus. That is because people who enter shopping sites like to see other products for sale. Amazon ads are no exception to the rule. Since it is one of the leading shopping sites in the world, creating ads on Amazon is an excellent way to introduce new customers to your product. And since you are already an Amazon FBA member, you can take advantage of the easy-access advertisements Amazon provides.

What Are Amazon Ads?

Amazon ads are paid, sponsored items that pop up as a result of keyword searches. When you search for an item on Amazon, the platform generates a paid advertisement that coincides with your search. For example, if you wanted to find a purple food that induced long episodes of laughter, you might find advertisements that correspond to "purple," "drink," or "laughter." In this case, the results yielded products related to food coloring and humorous mugs.

Ads are designed to optimize the results of Amazon searches, so be aware of the keywords you use when describing your product. Amazon will use those keywords to make the best possible matches with customer searches.

Are Amazon Ads Worth It?

Consider the last time you spent time on Amazon. Were you swayed by some of the advertisements listed on the home page, or did you make it to the advertisements listed on individual search pages? Either way, it is likely that you have clicked on an ad sometime in your experience with Amazon. So, is it worth it to advertise on Amazon when you have an FBA account? Absolutely! You are already set up with a platform that is designed to help you sell your products, so utilize all the tools that Amazon offers.

Ads generate more clicks for your products, and general studies have noted that interest in your products rises considerably when advertising with paid ads (Whitney, 2019). If you are a first-time seller and do not know where to start with paid advertisements, consult your market research to find trending products. Often, products with these advertisements will also give you a leg up in discovering your own methods for paid advertisements.

Amazon Advert Costs

Like most online advertisements these days, you can set a budget for your ad. That means that you can choose how much you want to spend and how much time your ad will run. So, if you decide to pay $5 over the course of one day, Amazon will provide you statistics that will let you know how many people you will reach on average. You can adjust your budget or day limit to make use of the estimated number of clicks.

On average, a click costs no more than $0.35. That means that your advertisement will bring a potential customer to your shop for every $0.35 you spend. That is a fairly good average, and it is a great way to get exposure.

Self-Serve Ads vs. Premium Ads

If you perform a Google search, you will likely see two different kinds of ads; one is listed among the options in the Google results, and the other is listed in the banner on the side or bottom of the page. Self-serve ads are those that are listed with the results. So, if you find yourself looking for a product with keywords similar to those searched, the advertisements would be listed on that page.

On the other hand, premium ads are usually those that have photographs and are glaringly obvious during a search or in search results.

For example, if you search for hyena products, you will undoubtedly find many people with interesting views of hyenas, but you might also see an advertisement for Blow Pops listed on the side, tempting you.

Types of Amazon Ads

Though we have discussed the styles of ads you might see when creating an ad with Amazon, there are three main types that you can select when advertising with Amazon. Each accepts payments with different methods, and each should be used according to different marketing strategies.

Amazon Sponsored Product Ads

These are the most common types of ads not only on Amazon, but also on the internet.

Customers navigate to your page by finding products within a search. As discussed previously, these ads respond to keywords, phrases, and lines. They correspond with links to specific products.

If you are new to Amazon selling, you may want to start with this option. Remember, you sell products, not themes. Once you sell your product efficiently, you can move on to more products. Sponsor your product by searching for common keywords used in competitor sites. Once you have decided on the keywords that best describe your product and get the most traffic, set up your sponsored product ad accordingly.

When paying for a sponsored product ad, you must set a daily budget. Again, you may choose the money you wish to put into an ad, but be smart when considering how many people the ad will reach. For example, if you set a high budget for a single day, you may find that the day you selected is not the best to sell your merchandise. Setting up an ad to sell paint on a Tuesday may be less effective than doing it on Thursday, since more people are interested in home projects on the weekends. Allow the two-day shipping time for the product to reach your customer and decide which time is best to sell your product.

Headline Search Ads

Headline search ads are often associated with links to other sites or company pages. For example, you may see a headline search ad for a whisk-making company located at the top of a page with search results for kitchen supplies. These ads are often available for a date in the future, so you have time to organize your advertisement and subsequent product before it is released. Headline search ads are also keyword based, so you will not see an ad for a cucumber slicer on the same page as a security system unless you have an abstract way of protecting your home.

This ad is a pay-per-click, which means that every click on the ad costs the company money. These ads are known as campaigns and have a minimum budget of $0.10 per keyword. You must pay at least $100 to display these ads, and the minimum cost per day is $1.00.

When it comes to marketing, you would often use these types of ads to inspire others to visit your shop. This suggests that you have a brand already set up with a variety of options. Unlike the sponsored product ads, you may advertise for your whole inventory, so use this ad when you have built up a good backing. Since the prices for running one of these ads are generally higher, be prepared to shell out a decent amount of money to run it.

Amazon Product Display Ads

The final type of Amazon ad is the product display ad. Unlike the other two, customers are led to various products through other product detail pages. If you visit Amazon and select a product, you will notice that the ads listed on the page often offer products that are similar to the products or include similar interests. For example, a runner looking for ankle weights might find an ad for running shoes. Amazon uses interests and keywords selected from a long list of options to provide the perfect example for all customers.

Using this ad is a good marketing technique for both new and seasoned sellers. The best way to utilize this type of ad is to do market research on the most common interests and uses for products related to yours. However, since there is a potential list from which to choose, your market research need not be as intense.

Instead, take some time reviewing products that are similar to yours.

How to Optimize Amazon Ads

Like the product listings, it is necessary to optimize Amazon ads to get the most out of your money. Optimizing ads is slightly different than providing keywords for your products, but they do have remarkable similarities. For both, you want to utilize the tools on Amazon to find the best companies to emulate, but instead of placing all keywords in your ad, you must bid on the best keywords. Some keywords are used frequently, so they often cost more than less-used versions. Always be aware of the best ways to show your products. Below are six ways to optimize your Amazon ads and make selling that much easier.

Organize Campaigns

It may seem like a no-brainer that you must organize how you will submit your campaigns, but there is often more to it than meets the eye. For example, not only do you have to find the best times to produce your ads, but you also must find the best words to use in your campaign. This is commonly called an AdWords account structure. You define the words that would most benefit your campaign and use them in advertising.

Let us look at an example. If you own a business that specializes in cell phone sales, you may have three main categories: Apple, Samsung, and Motorola. These three categories can be broken down even further to specialize in each brand. The Apple Brand may break down into iPhone X, iPhone 8, and iPhone 7. Samsung might have subcategories that include the Galaxy Note10, Galaxy S10, and the Galaxy

A20. Motorola may be divided into subcategories such as Moto G, Moto Z, and Moto One. All of these phones have their own subcategories, which may include storage, RAM, etc.

The breakdown of each of these categories provides its own unique set of keywords that can be utilized in ads. Create several ads that support each keyword to get the most exposure.

You will see an increase in sales if you research how much each keyword is used in popular sites. Visit well-known company sites and do a keyword search. Though many company pages will have some of the same keywords, sift through these to find keywords that will match your ad.

Create Compelling and Urgent Ad Copy

No one wants to read about a product that simply explains why the seller thinks the product is so great. Though it is a good idea to include details in your copy, remember that people from all walks of life will be reading it. You want to be able to reach as many people as possible in as short a time as possible. People are more likely to click on a product if they do not have to slog through all the literature.

Though you want to reach as wide an audience as possible, marketing in too wide a market will often result in fewer clicks as your copy does not answer questions about the product. Keywords come back as a seller's best friend because the more specific you can become with your copy, the more likely people are to see what you have to say.

Create an urgent desire for your product. If you are selling shoe inserts, find out the problems most people have with their shoes and capitalize on them. Advertising a shoe insert as a solution to bad posture may not seem like the best option, but advertising that the insert will help to solve back problems will encourage customers to visit your product's page. People looking for solutions to problems are more likely to write down the symptom than the remedy when searching for products.

Create Specific Ads

We cannot stress enough that being specific in your product descriptions and ads is one of the best ways to create an ad that will stick in customer's minds. Most people do not search the web by typing "yellow" into a Google search window. Buyers are looking for specific solutions to their problems.

Keywords such as "phone" or "paint" may put you on a search list, but you will likely only have the spot on the 1,000th page. Instead, consider narrowing the search area by adding adjectives and adverbs. For example, key phrases like "16GB phone" or "primer paint" narrow down the search considerably.

Bid on Popular Brands

It may seem overwhelming to compete with big-name brands such as Maybelline or North Face, but you can use these brands to get ahead in the advertising game. For example, instead of using words like "furniture," select a large brand like "IKEA." Since these brands are often at the top of lists, it is more likely that your brand name will appear with the big dogs.

If you have a rather specific niche and are looking for the top competitors for more unique items, simply type a general term into a search engine. The results will yield ads from other companies (good signs that they have enough cash flow to afford ads on Google searches) and you will likely find articles that rank the best brand names in the biz.

Experiment with Ad Formats

Though we have specified which marketing technique works with each of the brands, do not be afraid to experiment. In fact, spend your marketing time doing just that. Though it may seem as though product sponsored ads are the only way to go when marketing for the first time, try a different option and compare the results. You may find that you like one version over the other.

The different ad formats reach shoppers in different ways. For example, though some like to find the ads at the top of their list of results, others may find it more helpful to find another product by clicking on an ad within the product details. Use your experience and survey others to see what they look for in an ad.

Use Negative Keywords

Negative keywords prevent buyers from viewing your ad because it does not match the keyword. For example, if you were to sell hummingbird homes and someone searched for home interior, they may see your ad, which would be a waste of a click. Your ads are only shown to so many people, depending on your budget and time frame. To prevent this from happening, use negative keywords to prevent accidental clicks. You may choose the word "kitchen" or "bedroom" to exclude any searches that may contain those keywords.

Often, when you use negative keywords, you are inadvertently also preventing your products from showing up in large, generic searches, which may also save you a view. The ads you optimize through this method often are marketed for specific results, so choose your negative keywords wisely.

Conclusion

Amazon ads are some of the best utilized in the business, and since you are now a fully-fledged Amazon seller, take advantage of some of the best technology out there. Consider what you can do when you stake a place for yourself in one of the world's leading online shopping companies.

If you are concerned about whether you should advertise with Amazon ads, the answer is still a resounding yes! Not only could you get more bang for your buck by launching ads specific to your products, but you will also gain much-needed exposure. Remember that your products are only as valuable as you make them, so give them the star treatment.

There are three types of Amazon ads: sponsored product ads, headline search ads, and Amazon product display ads. Each is unique in its opportunity to reach several types of audiences. If you feel as though you are going to break the bank with this venture, do not worry. You can often choose the amount of money you want to spend on each ad and select the right time frame for you.

Optimizing ads, just like optimizing your products, is one of the most beneficial ways to encourage new customers to see your products. Make sure your ads are organized or you will never know which ads perform well for which products. Organize your ads into keyword research, and apply two or more ads to every subcategory to find out which type of ad works best. Remember, do not be afraid to experiment.

Be specific in your ads, and bring in the use of other brand names to make your brand pop. Even though you may not sell North Face jackets, you can always market your products as items similar to them. These specific keywords associated with big brands also narrow down the amount of general information customers have to sift through in order to find your product. The use of negative keywords also helps to prevent general terms from using your clicks.

Chapter 11: Creating Your Brand

Now that you have completed the setup and are on your way to creating a store that will be the envy of all other stores, the bulk of the hard work is done. All right, so the hard work is maintaining a profitable store on Amazon, but you have completed everything necessary for an excellent startup. The rest of the work comes through making your business stand the test of time.

Monitoring Your Amazon FBA Business

Even if you have automated the rest of your store, it is still necessary to make sure that everything is still in working order while you wander the beaches of the Bahamas. Below is a list of the most important parts of your business to monitor after you have completed the majority of the work.

Earnings

Though you may have found your time to shine in the halls of the Amazon FBA elite, you still need to regularly check your earnings. If you see the numbers start to slip, add more market research to your routine. Amazon has a detailed list of payment reports that are available to every Amazon FBA seller, so check the record frequently to see where you stand.

Fees

Though often thought of as the bane of the business existence, they are still a very active part of what you earn. If you notice an increase in fees, check your emails to find an Amazon email that will explain the change. Always remember that fees are subject to change at any time, and storage fees jump to more than three times the normal rate from October through December. Change your prices according to the changes in fees to allow for more profitable results.

Seller Rank

It is not enough to be a seller; you have to be the best seller on Amazon. Okay, so this can go too far in many ways, but always remember that your seller rank determines your profits. As you continue to grow your business, always strive to climb the ladder to become the best in your niche.

Also remember to score well with customers. Always respond to questions unanswered and make it a point to connect with your customers. Your overall rank will increase when customers are satisfied with your products.

Order Defect Rate

Always monitor the products that you send to the public. If you consistently send products that are damaged or otherwise impaired, you may suffer from a loss of understanding from Amazon. Amazon has been known to delete listings due to inferior products.

Perfect Order Percentage

This is mostly out of your hands since Amazon handles all the shipping and handling after you send them the product, but it is important to maintain a high percentage by keeping all inventory in stock and following up on orders that have been lost. If you receive a large percentage of lost packages, speak with Amazon and request information about the losses.

Customer Dissatisfaction Rate

The customers are your greatest asset when dealing with Amazon FBA. You want to make sure that they are happy with their products and will come back again and again. If you work within a commingling account, your dissatisfaction rate may increase due to other sellers who offer cheap products. Always stay a cut above the game by ensuring your customers are getting the right product by letting them know which brand to choose.

Pre-Fulfillment Cancellation Rate

The pre-fulfillment cancellation rate is completed by the seller who usually does not have enough inventory in stock. To prevent this from happening, always maintain a constant stream of stock headed to Amazon at all times. Amazon is very unforgiving when it comes to a low pre-fulfillment cancellation rate and only accepts a 2.5% window of failure. To find your rate, divide the number of orders you have canceled by the number of total products sold.

Conversion Rate

See how much your customer base changes over time by seeing how the numbers fluctuate between your store and others with similar products. Also, discover your conversion rate by comparing days, months, or weeks. Always use the same time period when calculating rates.

Conclusion

When starting your business, it is a good idea to get the most fundamental things out of the way, but when you are finished, it is important to keep an eye on your business to see where it is and is not growing. Be prepared to follow competitors and continue with your marketing every day to become a better seller with Amazon FBA. It is your responsibility to take care of your business, so make it a priority.

Take care to understand how your information is running from the most menial detail to the bigger picture. The only way to profit from your company is to keep an eye on your financials. This means that you must monitor your earnings every day. From fee deductions to loss of inventory, you need to know that you can still make a profit on the products you sell. Fees often sneak up on sellers if you do not know all of the fees involved. Refresh the fee policies often to make sure you understand all changes.

Though you do not have complete control over your seller rank, you must constantly monitor every comment made about your products to improve and build customer trust. Look to obtain a nearly perfect order percentage. If you forget about the products that need stocking, ask a third-party company to do the majority of the work for you. Though it may cost extra to get the best service, it may be worth it.

Make sure that customers understand when you are trying to fix an issue, and often communicate your apologies to customers who have received defective products. Your customers are the people that keep you in business, so monitor how you well you retain those customers. Be vocal and active with your products.

Conclusion

Amazon is one of the leading companies of online stores in the world, and it is easy to see why: They have products that many customers did not know they needed, and it is usually at an unbeatable price. Since its beginning, Amazon has been completely devoted to its loyal customer base, and it has only expanded the savings for loyal customers by offering incentives such as Amazon Prime.

With all the sales that Amazon generates every month, it only makes sense to take a part of that pie. After all, if anyone can learn this, you can. Third-party sellers make up more than half of the selling companies on Amazon, and they command a whopping three times the number of products. There is always room for more products in Amazon's massive warehouse collection, and you should be one of the many sellers who can make a living from selling products.

So, do you have what it takes? If you completed this book, then it is obvious that you do. The most difficult part of Amazon FBA is becoming a motivated seller that can take the frustration that may come from sales (or lack thereof) and turn it around. Even if you believe that this does not describe you, we promise that you can get there. All it takes is a little elbow grease and a lot of heart.

Why would you want to sign up with Amazon FBA when there are other options out there and you are just starting out? Amazon has created a third-party selling model that has inspired thousands of other businesses, and they have only refined their practices, so you know that you are getting the most out of the business.

Developing a mindset that will propel you through the most difficult times in your seller journey is absolutely vital. Luckily, we proved that you can find motivation in anything, even setbacks. Find only the best information on the internet and books and sift through the stuff that either makes you waste your time or ends up completely wrong. Believe us, we have seen both sides of that equation. As soon as you find your center with the right information, you can start to build your vision through careful planning and goals. Create your vision from your passions, and it will become easier to be motivated in the future. Once you have set up your goals, keep at them and renew them every time they expire. If you do not meet the goal you had hoped, try again. There is no expiration date for success.

Amazon is responsible for the majority of the work in your professional relationship, which frees up your time to do the things necessary to grow your business. As soon as you send your products to Amazon, they file your products away in a warehouse awaiting a customer. As soon as there is a bite, they send your product to the customer, all of which is done with the Prime shipping plan. Customers get two-day shipping and you get the peace of mind knowing that you did not have to do anything else. Amazon is in charge of customer service and your payment, and all you have to do is keep that inventory stocked for more customers.

Just as with any other company, there are advantages and disadvantages to working with Amazon FBA. If you like the idea of selling but do not want to handle all the customer interaction that goes with it, Amazon FBA is an excellent choice for you. They also offer discounted shipping rates for their professional account holders, which means you can ship packages to Amazon much cheaper than it would cost for you to send them out yourself. Amazon also manages all returns and customer complaints unless there is something wrong with the product. Amazon has potentially unlimited storage space (if you have the money to keep all of it stocked) and promises quick delivery to and from the Amazon warehouse. Amazon also includes a multi-channel fulfillment option that allows you to sell products from your own site.

However, if you are struggling with finances, the costs and fees are difficult to overcome, especially if your products simply sit on the shelves, not budging. Because Amazon promises free returns, you may also have to pay a fee for all customer returns, which can add up. When you create an account, you may have to handle difficult product preparation including obtaining a UPC code and handling all packaging. You are also responsible for the sales tax you receive from your sales. Though Amazon takes the taxes for you, they require that you pay them to all the states necessary, which can get hairy. Finally, commingling can be dangerous if you are not careful. Be sure to work with a company that offers quality products to prevent returns and bad customer reviews.

Set up a seller account with either an individual or a professional account. We recommend the individual account if you are just starting to sell with Amazon. If you are more accustomed to selling, take the plunge with a professional account. Not only will you receive more benefits, but you do not have to worry about Amazon's $1.00 fee for every product purchased. Remember to read all sections of your profile account to find the best information and change the wrong information before you start to sell to prevent a future headache.

When discovering the product that is perfect for you, remember that there is no such thing as a perfect product. Just choose a lucrative product and start selling! Engage your audience, friends, and family with surveys about products you would like to sell or those you have already sold. It is important to use the best information when setting up your own shop to prevent you from squandering your money on non-profitable products. Check out online resources to find a profitable product and then stick to it! You can grow your empire when you have mastered a single product.

Find your niche by looking through the products you are passionate about. If you find yourself passionate about more than one thing, use that information to better sell your product and move on to the next one. Avoid products that go in and out of season and instead settle for products that are useful and profitable all year long. Grow your marketing by creating videos and reviews for your products. Remember that the best products are those that are smaller because they are easier to handle and store. Create a place where you can search for your niche and enjoy the process.

Whether you choose wholesalers, overseas merchants, or a little bit of both, gain an understanding with your providers and open the lines of communication. Be an advocate for your product and the people with whom you work. Use your negotiation skills to find the best products at the best prices.

Create an optimized listing and ad by becoming aware of the product's features and dimensions. Instead of just putting yourself in your customer's shoes, put your customers in your shoes. Give them enough detail that they will know exactly what they need to know about the product. They can always ask you more questions later, but get as much detail onto the platform as possible. Use the ads within Amazon to guide customers to your site. You can use sponsored product ads, headline search ads, or product display ads, but do not just stop at one. Use all of your options to find out which one works for you.

Finally, always remember to monitor your account. Pay attention to your finances and always remember to put the customer first. They are the people that bring you success, and you should treat them like it.

With all the knowledge you have learned about Amazon FBA, do not be afraid to try out your own ideas and become the best seller on Amazon.

www.ingramcontent.com/pod-product-compliance
Lightning Source LLC
Chambersburg PA
CBHW070622220526
45466CB00001B/74